Mourning in the Mountains
Reflections on the Passing

David Chaltas

Mourning in the Mountains
Reflections on the Passing
Copyright: By David Chaltas 2006
1st Edition
ISBN: 978-0-6151-8436-4
Front & back cover photo: Morning on Pine
Mountain in Letcher County, Kentucky
Front & back cover photo: Courtesy Wayne Watts

Other books by the Author:
The Legend and Legacy of Lee
The Fading of the Gray
Poetry of the Civil War
Good Kids-Bad Behavior
Tears in the River
Just Over the Dawn
The Diaper Tree
Alpha and Omega of Sayings
Appalachian Expressions
Native American Sayings, Customs and Prayers
Confederate Kin
Appalachian Rebels
To Follow the Drums
The Search for Butternut

David Chaltas
Deer Branch Road
Box 41
Jeremiah, KY 41826
Lulu.com/davidchaltas

Printed in the United States of America

DEDICATION

To those that have gone before, may they rest in the shadow of the trees. To those crossing that great river, may you be blessed in the assurance that God will guide you as He did in your birth. For those awaiting the journey through that turbid vale, may you be prepared and greet the end with the joy of a new birth. To Michael Wright, who shared the joy of life as he fought gallantly the angel of death, I offer my salutations at redefining bravery. To my children, I offer my gratitude and undying devotion. I offer a special tribute to my mentor, hero, and friend, Sergeant Major Ben Buster Taylor, as he now rests in Arlington National Cemetery, Arlington, Virginia. To John Wesley Roark, I bid you safe journey brother and shall see you soon. To the Hospice movement, God will richly bless your love for your brothers and sisters. Finally, for those that cared to share their experiences, I thank you and know that your stories, poems, and words will help someone, as they embrace the final curtain.

TABLE OF CONTENTS

Mourning in the Mountains 5

Sayings of the Passing 8

Reflections of the Passing...69

Poems of the Passing 99

The Last Roll Call and Recovery................................111

Information of Customs/Rituals.................................114

Final Disposition...116

Customs of Major Religious Groups 118

Famous Epitaphs...125

Final Thoughts Via Sayings.......................................126

MOURNING IN THE MOUNTIANS

Nestled in the Appalachian Mountains and shadowed by the grandeur of their beauty dwell special people. They are people of traditions. Traditions are a mainstay of their lives. They treasure their traditions and rich heritage. They cling proudly to the old ways that they have embraced for hundreds of years. It is the way they do things. It is a way of life. It is a way of death. They laugh together and mourn together. They watch the sunrise, as they watch the sunset. They are united in joy as well as grief. They are the men and women of the mountains. They are Appalachians. They celebrate life in different ways. I am proud to count myself in their number. I am Appalachian and honored to be one fortunate enough to be known as one.

Our music, dance and culture ring with reflections of yesteryear. So is our way of mourning. Our rites of mourning are as unique as the mountains. We deal with death in the same manner that our ancestors did. We pay homage to the lost one and give our love and support to those left behind. I offer a brief look into mourning in the mountains along with offering words of wisdom to assist family members left behind. First are the sayings that I have collected over years, they serve as a means in which we can find solace, as we ponder upon the life changes that death has brought to our door. Next are reflections of the passing, they are personal narratives that some of my college students as well as public school students wished to contribute to help others during this period of bereavement. Reflections through poetry are gifts from some of my grade school, high school and college friends that wanted to share their time of despair with others going through that turbulent time of trouble and turmoil. The customs are a comparison of other rituals that are practiced across the world.

In the mountains of Eastern Kentucky, the practices of embalming and cremation are followed. Interment usually occurs in the family cemetery, surrounded by those loved ones that have gone before. The tradition of sitting up with the dead is still considered the standard for the old timers but the latest trend is to have the remains housed at a funeral parlor for viewing and visitation. 'Sitting up with the dead' began as a manner in which to ensure that the 'dead person' was truly dead (embalming was not practiced or required in several cases) and not in a coma or stupor. The purpose was to insure that he/she would not be buried alive.

The funeral consists of opening comments by the preacher, singing by the congregation gathered, preaching and eulogy. Reflections of the person that has passed are offered by the visitors and shared with each other. Food is usually available, as all pay their respect to the family and view the body of the loved one. In Eastern Kentucky it is traditional for the friends and family of the deceased to bring food and other items to the home. This is intended to relieve the family of the burden of food preparation during the initial mourning period.

The actual burial entails following the hearse to the gravesite and assisting in carrying the body to the hallowed ground where he/she will be interred.

There a brief graveside service is given and after prayer, the mourners are dismissed. The volunteers stay behind and assist in placing the coffin into the vault. The dirt is placed over the vault and smoothed over, with the flowers placed upon top of the grave.

Mourning in the Mountains shares the grief after the burial. Family and friends visit the home of the departed and offer support to them. They continue sharing the grief and offer their love in such a manner as to reduce the terrible pain of the loss. It is a mountain tradition to do so. It will continue to be so as long as we remember the old ways and share the morning as well as the mourning in the mountains with those that we love. So long as we remember, we will love...

SAYINGS OF THE PASSING

Over the years I have endeavored to capture sayings regarding the passing. Some sayings are from famous authors, poets and clergy. Some are simply individual's thoughts on the subject. All have value and are tools in dealing with death. In the mountains, my people are reflective and accepting of death as a natural part of life. We share and offer a helping hand simply by being there, saying something or just holding a person's hand, as they express their sorrow. I pray that the following quotes and sayings afford a sense of comfort.

"A bodily disease which we look upon as whole and entire within itself, may, after all, be but a symptom of some ailment in the spiritual part."
Nathaniel Hawthorne

"A candle loses nothing by lighting another candle."
Erin Majors

"A faithful friend is the medicine of life."
Ecclesiastes 6:16

"A friend of mine stopped smoking, drinking, overeating, and chasing women – all at the same time. It was a lovely funeral." *Unknown*

"A heart of gold stopped beating, two shining eyes at rest. God broke our hearts to prove He only takes the best." *Written For Michael Wright*

"A lizard continues its life into the wilderness like a human into heaven. Our fate is entirely dependent on our life." *Andrew Cornish*

"A man does not die of love or his liver or even of old age; he dies of being a man." *Percival Arland Ussher*

"A man is not completely born until he is dead." *Benjamin Franklin*

"A man's dying is more the survivor's affair than his own." *Thomas Mann*

"A man's ethical behavior should be based effectually on sympathy, education, and social ties; no religious basis is necessary. Man would indeed be in a poor way if he had to be restrained by fear of punishment and hope of reward after death." *Albert Einstein*

"A new idea is delicate. It can be killed by a sneer or a yawn; it can be stabbed to death by a joke or worried to death by a frown on the right person's brow." *Charles Brower*

"A person who chooses to die or to risk death demonstrates that there are values, principles, maxims, that are more valuable to him than life itself. In short, he places his immortal self above his mortal self. Nothing goes by luck in composition. It allows of no tricks. The best you can write will be the best you are." *Henry David Thoreau*

"A punishment to some, to some a gift, and to many a favor." *Seneca*

"A simple child that lightly draws its breath, and feels its life in every limb. What should it know of death?" *William Wordsworth*

"A single death is a tragedy, a million deaths is a statistic." *Unknown*

"A warrior thinks of death when things become unclear. The idea of death is the only thing that tempers our spirit." *Carlos Castaneda*

"A warrior considers himself already dead, so there is nothing to lose. The worst has already happened to him, therefore he's clear and calm; judging him by his acts or by his words, one would never suspect that he was witness to everything." *Carlos Castaneda*

"After I'm dead I'd rather have people ask why I have no monument than why I have one." *Cato the Elder (234-149 B.C.)*

"All are but the parts of one stupendous whole, whose body Nature is, and God the soul." *Alexander Pope*

"All God does is watch us and kill us when we get boring. We must never be boring." *Unknown*

"All God's giants have been weak men who did great things because they reckoned on His being with them." *James Hudson Taylor*

"All our knowledge merely helps us die a more painful death than animals that know nothing." *Maurice Masterlinck*

"All say, 'How hard it is that we have to die'; a strange complaint to come from the mouths of people who have had to live." *Mark Twain*

"Am I dying or is this my birthday?"
Lady Nancy Witcher Langhorne Astor

"Am I lightheaded because I'm not dead or because I'm still alive?" *Heidi Sandige*

"An English professor in college once told our class about how he dealt with the death of a close friend. He said he went home and played a recording of the saddest music he knew. He plunged into the darkness; he acknowledged his grief and allowed it to pour out. He knew that the only way he could get beyond his loss was to allow himself to feel the pain in all it's intensity." *Helen Luke in The Way of Woman*

"Ancient Egyptians believed that upon death they would be asked two questions and their answers would determine whether they could continue their journey in the afterlife. The first question was, 'Did you bring joy?' and the second was, 'Did you find joy?'" *Leo Buscaglia*

"And come he slow or come he fast it is but death who comes at last." *Unknown*

"And fear not them which kill the body; but are not able to kill the soul; but rather fear him which is able to destroy both body and soul in hell."
Matthew 10:28

"And I looked, and behold a pale horse: and his name that sat on him was Death." *Revelation 6: 8*

"And I will show that nothing can happen more beautiful than death." *Walt Whitman*

"And life is what we make it, always has been, always will be." *Grandma Moses*

"And the wild regrets and the bloody sweats, none knew so well as I. That he who lives more lives than one, more deaths than one shall die." *Oscar Wilde*

"And they die an equal death-the idler and the man of mighty deeds." *Homer, Iliad*

"And what the dead had no speech form when living, they can tell you, being dead: the communication of the dead is tongued with fire beyond the language of the living." *T. S. Eliot*

"Anything I've ever done that ultimately was worthwhile...initially scared me to death." *Betty Bender*

"Are small matters compared to what lies within us?" *Ralph Waldo Emerson*

"As a well-spent day brings happy sleep, so a life well used brings happy death." *Leonardo da Vinci*

"As death, when we come to consider it closely, is the true goal of our existence? I have formed during the last few years such close relations with this best and truest friend of mankind, that his image is not only no longer terrifying to me, is indeed very soothing and consoling! And I thank my God for graciously granting me the opportunity…of learning that death is the key which unlocks the door to our true happiness." *Thomas Mann*

"As in the eye of Nature he has lived, so in the eye of Nature let him die!" *William Wordsworth*

"As it is with a play, so it is with life – what matters is not how long the acting lasts, but how good it is." *Seneca*

"As men, we are all equal in the presence of death." *Publilius Syrus*

"As a well spent day brings happy sleep, so a life well used brings a happy death." *Leonardo de Vinci*

"As we look deeply within, we understand our perfect balance. There is no fear of the cycle of birth, life and death. For when you stand in the present moment, you are timeless." *Rodney Yee*

"Assassination has never changed the history of the world." *Disraeli*

"At the end of our life, we ought to be able to look back over it from our deathbed and know somehow the world is a better place because we lived, we loved, we were other-centered, other-focused." *Joe Erhmann, Football Coach*

"Because I could not stop for Death, he kindly stopped for me.   The Carriage held but just ourselves and immortality." *Emily Dickinson*

"Because I have loved life, I shall have no sorrow to die." *Amelia Burr*

"Be ashamed to die until you have won some victory for humanity." *Horace Mann*

"Be of good cheer about death and know this as a truth that no evil can happen to a good man, either in life or after death." *Jean Paul Richter*

"Be strong and of good courage, fear not, nor be afraid...for the lord thy God he it is that doth go with thee; he will not fail thee, nor forsake thee." *Deuteronomy*

"Be sure to live your life, because you are a long time dead."   *Scottish Proverb*

"Begin at once to live, and count each separate day as a separate life." *Seneca*

"Between grief and nothing I will take grief."
William Faulkner

"Beyond is an infinite morning of a day without tomorrow." *W. S. Abbott*

"But in the night of death hope sees a star, and listening love can hear the rustle of a wing." *Ingeresoll*

"Beginning today, treat everyone you met as if they were going to be dead by midnight. Extend to them all the care, kindness, and understanding you can muster, and do it with no thought of any reward. Your life will never be the same again." *Og Mandino*

"Birth and Death are the two noblest expressions of bravery." *Kahlil Gibran*

"Born free, taxed to death." *Unknown*

"But I will be, a bridegroom in my death, and run into as to a lover's bed." *William Shaksepeare*

"By faith we are conquerors of all things and hold within our hearts a promise of tomorrow." *Unknown*

"By the sweat of your brow you will eat your food until you return to the ground, since from it you were taken; for dust you are and to dust you will return." *Genesis 3*

Caterpillar to Butterfly

Caterpillar: "How do you become a butterfly?"
Butterfly: "You have to be willing to die."
Caterpillar: "Die?"
Butterfly: "Well, it feels like you are dying, but it really turns out to be a transformation to something better." *Unknown*

"Come lovely and soothing death, Undulate round the world, serenely arriving, arriving, in the day, in the night, to all, to each, Sooner or later, delicate death." *Walt Whitman*

"Cowards die many times before their deaths; the valiant never taste of death but once." *William Shakespeare*

"Curst be he that moves my bones." *William Shakespeare*

"Death and life were not till man made up the whole lock, stock, and barrel." *Unknown*

"Death and taxes and childbirth! There's never any convenient time for any of them." *Margaret Mitchell (Gone With the Wind)*

"Death borders upon our birth, and our cradle stands in the grave. Our birth is nothing but our death begun." *Bishop Hall*

"Death came with friendly care; the opening bud to heaven conveyed, and bade it blossom there." *Samuel Taylor*

"Death cannot stop true love. All it can do is...delay it for a while." *The Princess Bride*

"Death does not concern us, because as long as we exist, death is not here. And when it does come, we no longer exist." *Epicurus*

"Death ends a life, not a relationship." *Jack Lemmon*

"Death has to be waiting at the end of the ride before you truly see the earth, and feel your heart, and love the world." *Jean Anouilh*

"Death in itself is nothing: but we fear to be we know not what, we know not where." *John Dryden*

"Death, in its silent, sure march is fast gathering those whom I have longest loved, so that when he shall knock at my door, I will more willingly follow." *R. E. Lee*

"Death is a silent rumor to the young." *Andrew Rooney*

"Death is but the opening and closing of doors. It is only after we close the door to our mortal earthly life, that we can open the door to our eternal spiritual life." *William Dutton*

"Death is as sure for that which is born, as birth is for that which is dead. Therefore grieve not for what is inevitable." *Bhagavad Gita*

"Death is beautiful when seen to be a law, and not an accident-it is as common as life." *Henry David Thoreau in a letter to Ralph w. Emerson (March 11, 1842)*

"Death is but a path to be trod if man would ever pass to God." *T. Parnell*

"Death is but a shadow across the path to heaven." *Unknown*

"Death is feared as birth is forgotten." *Doug Horton*

"Death is for many of us the gate of hell; but we are inside on the way out, not outside on the way in." *George Bernard Shaw*

"Death is just a body problem." *Chuck Griswold*

"Death is life's way of telling you that you've been fired." *R.Geis*

"Death is more universal than life. Everyone dies but not everyone lives." *A. Sachs*

"Death is not extinguishing the light; it is putting out the lamp because dawn has come." *Rahindranth Tagore*

"Death is not the foe, but an inevitable adventure." *Sir Oliver Lodge*

"Death is not the greatest loss in life. The greatest loss is what dies inside us while we live." *Norman Cousins*

"Death is nothing else but going home to God, the bond of love will be unbroken for all eternity." *Mother Teresa*

"Death is nothing to us, since when we are, death has not come, and when death has come, we are not." *Epicurus*

"Death is one of the few things that can be done as easily as lying down. The difference between sex and death is that with death you can do it alone and no one is going to make fun of you." *Woody Allen*

"Death is one of two thing. Either it is annihilation, and the dead have no consciousness of anything; or, as we are told, it is really a change: a migration of a soul from one place to another." *Socrates*

"Death is only the embracement of God to his children." *Unknown*

"Death is our eternal companion. It is always to our left, an arm's length behind us." *Carlos Castaneda*

"Death is the only wise advisor that a warrior has. Whenever he feels that everything is going wrong and he's about to be annihilated, he can turn to his death and ask if that is so. His death will tell him, I haven't touched you yet." *Carlos Casteneda*

"Death is patiently making my mask as I sleep. Each morning I awake to discover in the corners of my eyes the small tears of his wax." *Philip Dow*

" ...Death is the destiny of every man..." *Ecclesiastes 7:2 NIV*

"Death is the dialogue between The Spirit and the Dust." *Emily Dickinson*

"Death is the golden key that opens the palace of Eternity." *Milton*

"Death is the king of this world: Tis his park where he breeds life to feed him. Cries of pain are music for his banquet." *George Eliot*

"Death is more universal than life; everyone dies but not everyone truly lives." *A. Sachs*

"Death is no more than passing from one room into another. But there's a difference for me, you know. Because in that other room I shall be able to see." *Helen Keller*

"Death is the most beautiful adventure in life." *Charles Frohman*

"Death is nature's way of saying, your table's ready." *Robin Williams*

"Death is nothing to us, since when we are, death has not come, and when death has come, we are not." *Epicurus*

"Death is the most beautiful adventure in life." *Charles Frohman*

"Death is the only inescapable, unavoidable, sure thing. We are sentenced to die the day we are born." *Gary Mark Gilmore*

"Death is the peak of a life-wave, and so is birth. Death and birth are one." *Abba Silver*

"Death is the veil which those who live call life: they sleep, and it is lifted." *Unknown*

"Death lies on her, like an untimely frost upon the sweetest flower of all the field." W. Shakespeare

"Death like birth is a secret of Nature." *Marcus A. Antonius*

"Death may be the greatest of all human blessings." *Socrates*

"Death row is a state of mind." *Doris Ann Foster*

"Death smiles at us all; all a man can do is smile back." *The movie: Gladiator*

"Death-the last sleep? No, it is the final awakening." *Unknown*

"Death, the sable smoke where vanishes the flame."

George Gordon, Lord Bryon, Childe Harold's Pilgrimage

"Death Valley is neither dead nor a valley." *Jerry Bunin, News Editor, Five Cities Times-Recorder, April 6, 1988*

"Death? Why this fuss about death? Use your imagination, try to visualize a world without death! Death is the essential condition of life, not an evil." *Charlotte Perkins Gilman*

"Desire is half of life, indifference is half of death." *Kahlil Gibran*
.

"Die happily and look forward to taking up a new and better form. Like the sun, only when you set in the west can you rise in the east." *Jelauddin Rumi*

"Die of a rose in aromatic pain*." Alexander Pope*

"Don't ask the doctor; ask the patient." *Yiddish Proverb*

"Don't cry because it's over; smile because it happened." *Unknown*

"Don't judge each day by the harvest you reap, but by the seeds you plant." *Robert Louis Stevenson*

"Don't take life too seriously because you can't come out of it alive." *Warren Miller*

"Do not act as if you would live ten thousand years. Death hangs over you." *Marcus Aurelius*

"Do not fear death so much, but rather the inadequate life." *Bertolt Brecht*

"Do not seek death. Death will find you. But seek the road which makes death a fulfillment." *Dag Hammarskjold*

"Do not take thought for your persons or your properties, but first and chiefly to care about the greatest improvement of the soul. I tell you that the virtue is not given by money, but that from virtue comes money and every other good of man, public as well as private. The difficulty, my friends, is not in avoiding death, but in avoiding unrighteousness; for that runs faster than death." *Sacrates*

Do ye hear the children weeping, O my brothers?" *Elizabeth Barrett Browning*

"Dream as if you will live forever. Live as if you will die today." *James Dean*

"Dust thou art, to dust returnest, was not spoken of the soul." *Longfellow*

"Dying is a wild night and a new road." *Emily Dickenson*

"Dying is a very dull, dreary affair. And my advice to you is to have nothing whatever to do with it." *W. Somerset Maugham*

"Dying seems less sad than having lived too little." *Gloria Steinem*

"Each departed friend is a magnet that attracts us to the next world." *Jean Paul Richter*

"Each man's life is but a breath." *Psalm 39*

"Each of us stands alone in this vast world, momentarily bathed in a ray of sunlight. And suddenly it's night." A line from *Quasimodo's poem, Ede Subito Sera*

"Earth has no sorrow that heaven can not heal." *Moore*

"Enjoy life. There's plenty of time to be dead." *Unknown*

"Eternal nothingness is fine if you happen to be dressed for it." *Woody Allen*

"Even at our birth, death does but stand aside a little. And every day he looks towards us and muses somewhat to himself whether that day or the next he will draw nigh" *Robert Bolt*

"Even death is not feared by one who has lived wisely." *Buddha*

"Even now I am full of hope, but the end lies with God." *Pindar*

"Every day, therefore, should be regulated as if it were the one that brings up the rear, the one that rounds out and completes our lives." *Seneca*

"Every man dies. Not every man really lives." *William Wallace, Braveheart*

"Every man's life is a plan of God." *Horace Bushnell*

"Every moment of one's existence one is growing into more or retreating into less. One is always living a little more or dying a little bit." *Norman Miller*

"Everybody wants to go to heaven, but nobody wants to die." *Unknown*

"Everyone is so afraid of death, but the real Sufis just laugh: nothing tyrannizes their hearts. What strikes the oyster shell does not damage the pearl." *Mevlana Rumi*

"Everything is drive-through. In California, they even have a burial service Jump-In-The-Box." *Wil Shriner*

"Faith builds a bridge across the gulf of death." *Young*

"Father into thine hands I commend my spirit."
Luke 23: 46 the *last words of Christ on the Cross*

"Fear, if allowed free rein, would reduce all of us to trembling shadows of men, for whom only death could bring release." *John M. Wilson*

"Fear not death, for the sooner we die the longer we shall be immortal." *Benjamin Franklin*

"Finish each day and be done with it. You have done what you could; some blunders and absurdities have crept in; forget them as soon as you can. Tomorrow is a new day; you shall begin it serenely and with too high a spirit to be encumbered with your old nonsense." *Ralph Waldo Emerson*

"First they ignore you, then they laugh at you, then they fight you, then you win." *Mahatma Gandhi*

"For death begins with life's first breath, and life begins at touch of death." *William Penn*

"For death is no more than a turning of us over from time to eternity." *William Penn*

"For God so loved the world that He gave His only begotten son, that whosoever believeth in Him shall not perish but have everlasting life." *John 3:16*

"For I am convinced that neither death nor life, neither angels nor demons, neither the present nor the future, nor any posers, neither height nor depth, nor anything else in all creation, will be able to separate us from the love of God that is in Christ Jesus our Lord." *Romans 8*

"For if he like a madman lived, At least he like a wise one died." *Cervantes*

"For in that sleep of death, what dreams may come." *William Shakespeare Hamlet*

"For life in the present there is no death. Death is not an event in life. It is not a fear in the world." *Willgenstein*

"For some, life lasts a short while, but the memories it holds last forever." *Laura Swenson*

"For the wages of sin is death; but the gift of God is eternal life though Jesus Christ our Lord."
Romans 6:23

"For what is it to die, but not to stand in the sun and melt into the wind? And when the Earth has claimed our limbs, then we shall truly dance." *Kahlil Gibran*

"For whosoever shall call upon the name of the Lord shall be saved." *Romans 10:13*

"Friends applaud, the comedy is over." *Beethoven's last words*

"From my rotting body, flowers shall grow and I am in them and that is eternity." *Edvard Munch*

"From a proud tower in the town, Death looks gigantically down." *Edgar Allan Poe*

"From the light we have come and to the light we shall return." *Josaine Antonette*

"From dust you are and to dust you will return." *Genesis 3:19*

"Give sorrow words; the grief that does not speak whispers the o'er fraught heart and bids it break." *Shakespeare*

"Good men must die, but death can not kill their names." *Spanish Proverb*

"God grant me the serenity to accept the things I can not change, the courage to change the things I can, and the wisdom to know the difference." *Reinhold Neibuhr*

"God has chosen her as a pattern for other angels. As you look at your own life, how might you be an angel to others? How might you pattern your life so as to inspire others to greater heights in their own loving and giving?" *Epitaph in an English Churchyard*

"God is and all is well." *Whittier*

"God is our refuge and strength, a very present help in trouble." *Psalms 46:1*

"God made death so we'd know when to stop." *Steven Stiles*

"God pours life into death and death into life without a drop being spilled." *Unknown*

"God's finger touched him, and he slept." *Alfred, Lord Tennyson*

"Goodbye, proud world! I'm going home; Thou art not my friend; I am not thine." *Ralph Waldo Emerson*

"Grief as I read somewhere once, is a lazy Susan. One day it is heavy and underwater, and the next day it spins and stops loud and rageful, and the next day at wounded keening, and the next numbness, silence." *Annie Lamott in Traveling Mercies*

"Grief is like the wind. When it's blowing hard, you adjust your sails and run before it. If it blows too hard, you stay in the harbor, close the hatches and don't take calls. When it's gentle, you go sailing, have a picnic, and take a swim." *Barbara Lazear Ascher in Landscape Without Gravity: A Memoir of Grief*

"Grief is a sign that we loved something more than ourselves...Grief makes us worthy to suffer with the rest of the world." *Joan Chittister in Gospel Days*

"Grief is love not wanting to let go." *Earl A. Grollman in Living with Loss*

"Grief is the time when we are blessed with the opportunity to complete a natural process of spiritual death and rebirth before our own death." *Stephanie Ericsson in Through the Darkness*

"Grief seems to me like a winter house: guarded, sheltered against an outside world that's expected to be difficult. The windows are small to keep out the cold, and little light gets in. The darkness and warmth make a cozy place to hide, to nurse wounds, to incubate what is not yet ready to be exposed," *Janet Cedar Spring in* Take Up Your Life

"Health is simply the absence of sickness." *Hannah Green*

"He had decided to live forever or die in the attempt." *J. Heller*

"He hath awakened from the dream of life." *Shelley*

"He is now at rest, and we who are left are the ones to suffer." *General Lee speaking on the death of General A. P. Hill*

"He is one of those people who would be enormously improved by death." *Hector Munro (1870-1916)*

"He now rests in the land that he loved." *President Jefferson Davis eulogy honoring General Lee*

"He sleeps a thousand deaths but only passed through one." *Author's comment in a speech about General Lee's dreams about his men*

"He who doesn't fear death dies only once." *Giovanni Falcone*

"He who has gone, so we but cherish his memory, abides with us, more potent, nay, more present than the living man." *Antoine de Saint-Exupery*

"He who knoweth how to suffer will enjoy much peace. Such a one is a conqueror of himself and the lord of the world, a friend of Christ and an heir of heaven." *Thomas ' Kempis*

"He thought it happier to be dead, to die for Beauty, than live for bread." *Ralph Waldo Emerson*

"He who dies with the most toys is, nonetheless dead." *Unknown*

"Healthy children will not fear life if their elders have integrity enough not to fear death."
Erik Erikson

"Heaven, the treasury of everlasting joy."
Shakespeare

"Here is the test to find whether your mission on Earth is finished: if you're alive it isn't." *Richard Back*

"Hold the cross high so I can see it through the flames." *Joan of Arc*

"Hope is the thing with feathers. That perches in the soul, and sings the tune without the words, and never stops at all." *Emily Dickinson*

"Hope is the companion of power and the mother of success. For those of us who hope the strongest have within us the gift of miracles." *Sydney Bremer*

"Hope, that with honey blends the cup of pain." *Sir William Jones*

"How vain it is to sit down to write when you have not stood up to live." *Henry David Thoreau*

"How soon faded the tender flower." *On Tombstone*

"I am become death, shatterer of worlds." *J. Robert Oppenheimer, upon witnessing the explosion of the first atomic bomb*

"I see Hermes, unsuspected, dying, well-beloved, saying to the people, "Do not weep for me, this is not my true country, I have lived banished from my true country – I now go back there, I return to the celestial sphere where every one goes in his turn." *Walt Whitman*

"I am ready to meet my Maker. Whether my Maker is prepared for the great ordeal of meeting me is another matter." *Winston Churchill*

"I'm not afraid of death. It's the stake one puts up in order to play the game of life." *Jean Giranudoux, Amphitryon, 1929*

"I believe that imagination is stronger than knowledge, that myth is more potent than history. I believe that dreams are more powerful than facts-that hope always triumphs over experience-that laughter is the only cure for grief. And I believe that love is stronger than death." *From the movie The Crow*

"I believe that when death closes our eyes we shall awaken to a light of which our sunlight is but the shadow." *Arthur Schopenhauer*

"I believe there are angels among us, sent down to us, from somewhere up above. They come to you and me, in our darkest hour, to show us how to give, teach us how to live, and guide us with the light of love." *Unknown*

"I believe there are two sides to the phenomenon known as death, this side where we live, and the other side where we shall continue to live. Eternity does not start with death. We are in eternity now." *Norman Vincent Peale*

"I cannot express the anguish I feel at the death of our sweet Annie. To know that I shall never see her again on earth, that her place in our circle, which I always hoped one day to enjoy, is forever vacant, is agonizing in the extreme. But God in this, as in all things, has mingled mercy with the blow, in selecting that one best prepared to leave us. May you be able to join me in saying, 'His will be done!'...I know how much you will grieve and how much she will be mourned. I wish I could give you any comfort, but beyond our hope in the great mercy of God, and the belief that He takes her at the time and place when it is best for her to go, there is none. May that same mercy be extended to us all, and may we be prepared for His summons." *Mrs. Mary Custis Lee speaking on the death of her daughter Annie.*

"I could not stop something I knew was wrong and terrible. I had an awful sense of powerlessness." *Andrei Sakharov*

"I didn't attend the funeral, but I sent a nice letter saying I approved of it." *Mark Twain*

"I do not believe that any man fears to be dead, but only the stroke of death." *Francis Bacon*

"I do not dread the kiss of death but neither do I run to its embrace." *David Chaltas*

"I existed from all eternity and, behold, I am here, and I shall exist till the end of time, for my being has no end." *Kahlil Gibran*

"I had it all, and I blew it." *Mickey Mantle (Shortly before dying from cancer and other complications of alcoholism)*

"I have died many a death in love, and yet, had not loved I would never have lived at all." *David Lasater*

"I have fought the good fight, I have finished the race, I have kept the faith." *2 Timothy 4:7*

"I have never killed a man, but I have read many obituaries with great pleasure." *Clarence Darrow*

"I heard yesterday, my dear daughter, with the deepest sorrow of the death of your infant. I was so grateful at her birth. I felt that she would be such a comfort to you, such a pleasure to my dear Fitzhugh, and would fill so full the void still aching in your hearts. But you have now two sweet angels in heaven. What joy there is in the thought. What relief to your grief. What suffering and sorrow they have escaped. I can say nothing to soften the anguish you must feel, and I know you are assured of my deep and affectionate sympathy. May God give you strength to bear the affliction. He has imposed and produced future joy out of present misery, is my earnest prayer. *R. E. Lee to his daughter-in -Law*

"I know death has ten thousand doors for men to take their exits." *John Webster*

"I know not what course others may take, but as for me, give me liberty or give me death." *Patrick Henry*

"I love the man that can smile in trouble, that can gather strength from distress, and grow brave by reflection. 'Tis the business of little minds to shrink, but he whose heart is firm, and whose conscience approves his conduct, will pursue his principles unto death." *Thomas Paine*

"I saw F (Fitzhugh) yesterday. He is well and wants much to see you. When you are strong enough, cannot you come up to Hickory Hill, or your grandpa's, on a little visit, where he could ride down and see you? My horse is waiting at my tent door, but I could not refrain from sending these few lines to recall to you the thought and love of your devoted father, R. E. Lee." *While still staggered by the loss of his daughter, General Lee received word of another personal loss, his granddaughter. In his letter dated December 10, 1862, he laments her untimely death but offers words of comfort.*

"I see that I am to wait for what will be exhibited by death." *Walt Whitman*

"In His will is our peace." *Dante*

"I only remember two kisses-the first and the last. The first, with my love and the last, with death. The first brought happiness and the last relief! *Srijit Prabhakaran*

"I shall not die of a cold. I shall die of having lived." *Willa Cather*

"I shall pass through this world but once. Any good, therefore, that I can show to any human being, let me do it now. Let me not defer nor neglect it, for I shall not pass this way again." *Stephen Grellet*

"I said to Life, I would hear Death speak. And Life raised her voice a little higher and said, 'You hear him now.'" *Kahlil Gibran*

"I see Hermes, unsuspected, dying, well-beloved, saying to the people, Do not weep for me, this is not my true country, I have lived banished from my true country – I now go back there, I return to the celestial sphere where every one goes in his turn." *Walt Whitman*

"I walked a mile with Sorrow and ne'er a word said she; but, oh, the things I learned from her when Sorrow walked with me." *Robert Browning*

"I wanted a perfect ending. Now I've learned, the hard way, that some poems don't rhyme, and some stories don't have a clear beginning, middle, and end. Life is about not knowing, having to change, taking the moment and making the best of it, without knowing what's going to happen next. Delicious ambiguity." *Gilda Radner*

"I went to the woods because I wished to live deliberately, to front only the essential facts of life and see if I could not learn what they had to teach; and not, when I came to die, discover that I had not lived." *Henry David Thoreau*

"I would die happy if I knew that on my tombstone could be written these words. This man was an absolute fool. None of the disastrous things that he reluctantly predicted ever came to pass!" *Lewis Mumford*

"I would rather die a meaningful death than to live a meaningless life." *Corazon Aquino*

"I would rather live and love where death is king than have eternal life where love is not." *Robert G. Ingersoll*

"I wouldn't mind dying – it's the business of having to stay dead that scares the crap out of me." *R. Geis*

"If I think more about death than some other people, it is probably because I love life more than they do." *Angelina Jolie*

"I'd rather die while I'm living than live while I'm dying." *Jimmy Buffet*

"If man hasn't discovered something that he will die for he isn't fit to live." *Martin Luther King*

"If man were immortal he could be perfectly sure of seeing the day when everything in which he had trusted should betray his trust, and, in short, of coming eventually to hopeless misery. He would break down, at last, as every good fortune, as every dynasty, as every civilization does. In place of this we have death." *Charles S. Peirce*

"If you're going through hell, keep going." *Sir Winston Churchill (1874-1965)*

"I'm not afraid of death. It's the stake one puts up in order to play the game of life." *Jean Giranudoux, Amphitryon, 1929*

"I'm not afraid to die, I just don't want to be there when it happens." *Unknown*

"Impossible is a word to be found only in the dictionary of fools." *Unknown*

"In the democracy of the dead all men at last are equal. There is neither rank nor station nor prerogative in the republic of the grave." *John James Ingalls*

"In the Midst of movement and chaos, keep stillness inside of you." *Deepak Chopra*

"In this world, nothing is for certain but death and taxes." *Benjamin Franklin*

"In the world to come, I shall not be asked, 'Why were you not Moses?' I shall be asked, 'Why were you not Zusya?'" *Rabbi Zusya*

"In three words I can sum up everything I have learned about life: It goes on." *Robert Frost*

"Into thine hand I commit my spirit, thou hast redeemed me, O Lord God of truth." *Psalms 31:5*

"Is death the last sleep? No- it is the last and final awakening." *Sir Walter Scott*

"It costs me never a stab nor squirm to thread my chance upon a worm. Aha, my little dear I say your clan will pay me back one day." *Unknown*

"It is a far, far better thing that I do, than anything I have ever done; it is a far, far, better rest that I go, than I have ever known." *Charles Dickens*

"It is better to die on your feet than live on your knees." *Emiliano Zapatta*

"It is foolish and wrong to be afraid of death. JUST THINK! No more repaired tires on the body vehicle, no more patchwork living." *Paramhausa Yogauauda*

"It is foolish and wrong to mourn the men who died. Rather we should thank God that such men lived." *George S. Patton, Jr.*

"It is God's love for us that sends us on our journey and it is our love for God that allows us to return to God's loving arms again." *David Goines*

"It is love, not reason, that is stronger than death." *Thomas Mann*

"It is more difficult, and it calls for higher energies of soul, to live a martyr than to die one." *Horace Mann*

"It is not all life to live, nor yet all of death to die. For life and death are one, and only those who will consider the experience as one may come to understand or comprehend what peace indeed means." *Edgar Cayce*

"It is not "anti-choice" and "pro-choice" it is pro-life" and "pro-death." *Unknown*

"It is not length of life, but depth of life." *Ralph Waldo Emerson*

"It is only when we truly know and understand that we have a limited time on earth, and that we have no way of knowing when our time is up, that we will begin to live each day to the fullest, as if it was the only one we had." *Elizabeth Kubler-Ross*

"It is only with the heart that one can see rightly. What is essential is invisible to the eye." *Antoine de Saint-Exupery*

"It is possible to provide security against other ills, but as far as death is concerned, we men live in a city without walls." *Epicurus*

"It is worth dying to find out what life is." *T. S. Eliot*

"It's a phony issue. To pretend the death penalty is going to end crime in the United States is to fool people, to promote public ignorance." *Rudolph W. Giuliani, former U.S. Attorney of New York, former mayor of New York City*

"It's impossible to experience one's death objectively and still carry a tune." *Woody Allen*

"It's not catastrophes, murders, deaths, diseases, that age and kill us; it's the way people look and laugh, and run up the steps of omnibuses." *Virginia Woolf*

"It's not the rules and regulations you follow carefully that will win you a favor with God but rather offering your life to Him in complete faith that His Son, Jesus Christ, conquered sin and death on your behalf and for your salvation." *James L. Matthews*

"It's not the tears that fall from the eyes and cover face that matter. It's the tears that fall from the heart and cover the soul." *Unknown*

"Jesus' parable of the prodigal son is the cosmic tale of each and every human being. We have all forgotten that we are children of God and that our spiritual side needs to return to God." *Dr. George Ritchie*

"Joy, joy forever! My task is done-the gates are pass'd and heaven is won." *Moore*

"Keep away form people who try to belittle your ambitions. Small people always do that, but the really great ones make you feel that you too, can become great." *Mark Twain*

"Knowledge by suffering entereth, and life is perfected by death." *Elizabeth B. Browning*

"Let us endeavor to live that when we come to die even the undertaker will be sorry." *Mark Twain*

"Let the soul be joyful in the present, distaining anxiety for the future, and tempering bitter things with a serene smile." *Horace*

"Learn as if you were going to live forever. Live as if you were going to die tomorrow." *Mahatma Gandhi*

"Lend, lend your wings! I mount! I fly! O grave! Where is thy victory? O death! Where is thy sting?" *Alexander Pope*

"Let us cross over the river and rest under the shade of the trees." *Stonewall Jackson on his deathbed*

"Life and death are balanced on the edge of a razor." *Homer, Iliad*

"Life does not cease to be funny when people die any more than it ceases to be serious when people laugh." *George Bernard Shaw*

"Life is a great sunrise. I do not see why death should not be an even greater one." *Vladimir Nobokov*

"Life is eternal and love is immortal; and death is only a horizon, and a horizon is nothing save the limit of our sight." *Rossiter W. Raymond*

"Life is pleasant. Death is peaceful. It's the transition that's troublesome." *Jimi Hendrix*

"Life without a friend is death without a witness."
Eugene Benge

"Love never dies a natural death. It dies because we don't know how to replenish its source. It dies of blindness and errors and betrayals. It dies of illness and wounds; it dies of weariness, of witherings, of tarnishings." *Unknown*

(Letcher County Miners' Memorial)

"Make sure to send a lazy man the angel of death."
Jewish Proverb

"Man does not live for himself alone in this mortal body, in order to work on its account, but also for all men on earth; nay, he lives only for others, and not for himself." *Martin Luther*

"Man's reach should exceed his grasp, or what's a heaven for." *Robert Browning*

"May you live all the days of your life." *Jonathan Swift*

"Men fear death, as children fear to go in the dark; and as that natural fear in children is increased with tales, so is the other." *Francis Bacon*

"Men fear death, as if unquestionably the greatest evil, and yet no man knows that it may not be the greatest good." *William Mitford*

"Men fear death, as children fear to go in the dark; and as the natural fear in children is increased with tales, so is the other." *Francis Bacon*

"Men that do not fear death either do not embrace life or they lie to themselves." *D. Chaltas*

"Mexico? Where life is cheap, death is rich, and the buzzards are never unhappy." *Unknown*

"Millions long for immortality who do not know what to do with themselves on a rainy Sunday afternoon." *Susan Ertz, Anger in the Sky*

"Music, when soft voices die, vibrates in the memory." *Shelley*

"Must not all things at the last be swallowed up in death?" *Plato*

"My life seems like one long obstacle course, with me as the chief obstacle." *Jack Paar*

"Neither fire nor wind, birth nor death can erase our good deeds." *Buddha*

"No bond in closer union knits to human hearts than fellowship in grief." *Robert Southey in <u>Joan of Arc and Minor Poems</u>*

"No gift is more needed by a dying world than a living Savior." *Unknown*

"No heaven can come to us unless our hearts find rest in it today." *Fra Giovanni*

"No matter how rich you become, how famous or powerful, when you die the size of your funeral will still pretty much depend on the weather." *Michael Pritchard*

"No one can confidently say that they will be living tomorrow." *Euripides*

"No one knows whether death is really the greatest blessing a man can have, but they fear it is the greatest curse, as if they knew well." *Plato*

"No taxation without respiration." *Rep. Bob Schaffer, R-Colorado, on repeal of the death tax.*

"Normally, we do not like to think about death. We would rather think about life. Why reflect on death? When you start preparing for death you soon realize that you must look into your life now and come to face the truth of your self. Death is like the true meaning of life is reflected." *Sogyal Rinpoche*

"Nothing can happen more beautiful than death." *Walt Whitman*

"Nothing in life is certain except death and taxes." *Ben Franklin*

"Nothing is certain but death and taxes. Of the two, taxes happen annually." *Joel Fox*

"Nothing makes a man more aware if his capabilities and of his limitations than those moments when he must push aside all the familiar defenses of ego and vanity, and accept reality by staring, with the fear that is normal to a man in combat, into the face of Death." *Major Robert S. Johnson, USAAF*

"Now he belongs to the angels." Later changed to, "Now he belongs to the ages." *Words spoken by the Secretary of State upon the death of Lincoln*

"Now twilight lets her curtain down and pins it with a star." *L.M. Child*

"Of all sad words of tongue or pen the most destructive are: 'If only I had.'" *Anonymous*

"O Captain? My Captain! Our fearful trip is done! The ship has weathered every rack, the prize we sought is won, the port is near, the bells I hear, the people all exalting." *Walt Whitman*

"Of course you don't die. Nobody dies. Death doesn't exist. You only reach a new level of vision, a new realm of consciousness, a new unknown world." *Henry Miller*

"Oh God, to have reached the point of death without ever having lived at all." *Thoreau*

"Old age was simply a delightful time, when the old people sat on the sunny doorsteps, playing in the sun with the children until they fell asleep. At last, they failed to wake up." *Jaytiamo*

"One hundred years from now, it will not matter what my bank account was, how big my house was, or what kind of car I drove. But the world may be a little better, because I was important in the life of a child." *Forest Witcraft*

"One must wait until evening to see how splendid the day has been." *Will Rogers*

"One owes respect to the Living. To the Dead, one owes only truth." *Voltaire*

"One should die proudly, when it is no longer possible to live proudly." *Nietzsche*

"Only nature has a right to grieve perpetually, for she only is innocent. Soon the ice will melt, and the blackbirds sing along the river, which he frequented as pleasantly as ever. The same everlasting serenity will appear in this face of God, and we will not be sorrowful, if he is not." *Henry David Thoreau (upon the death of his brother)*

"Only the destructive forces know death as lord. Only spiritual forces know life as the Lord. Know ye the Lord!" *Edgar Cayce*

"Only those that dared to let go can dare to reenter." *Meister Eckhart*

"Our birth is nothing but our death begun." *Edward Young, Night Thoughts*

"Our brains are seventy-year clocks. The Angel of Life winds them up once for all, then closes the case, and gives the key into the hand of the Angel of the Resurrection." *Oliver Wendell Holmes*

"Our Construction is in actual operation; everything appears to promise that it will last; but in this world nothing is certain but death and taxes." *Benjamin Franklin*

"Our care should not be to have lived long as to have lived enough." *Seneca*

"Our death is not an end if we can live on in our children and the younger generation. For they are us, our bodies are only wilted leaves on the tree of life." *Einstein*

"Our fear of death is like our fear that summer will be short, but when we have had our swing of pleasure, our fill of fruit, and our swelter of heat we say we have had our day." *Ralph Waldo Emerson*

"Our life is a flying shadow, God the pole, the needle pointing to Him is our soul." *Unknown*

"Our life is made by the death of others." *Unknown*

"Pale death with an impartial foot knocks at the hovels of the poor and the palaces of kings." *Horace*

"Pain past is pleasure." *Thomas Fuller*

"Paradise-I see flowers from the cottage where I lie." *Yaitsu's death poem, 1807*

"People are like stained glass windows. The true beauty can be seen only when there is light from within. The darker the night, the brighter the windows." *Elizabeth Kubler-Ross*

"People living deeply have no fear of death." *Anais Nin, Diary, 1967*

"People may not remember exactly what you did or what you said, but they will always remember how you made them feel." *Unknown*

"Perhaps passing through the gates of death is like passing quietly through the gate in a pasture fence. On the other side, you keep walking, without the need to look back. No shock, no drama, just the lifting of a plank or two in a simple wooden gate in a clearing. Neither pain, nor floods of light, nor great voices, but just the silent crossing of a meadow." *Mark Helprin; A Soldier of the Great War*

"Praise be the fathomless universe, for life and joy and for objects and knowledge curious; and for love, sweet love – but praise! O praise and praise, for the sure-enwinding arms of cool-enfolding Death." *Walt Whitman*

"Precious in the sight of the LORD is the death of His saints." *Psalms 116*

"Rattling the chains of death should never silence the sound of life." *David Chaltas*

"Recall your courage, and lay aside sad fear." *Virgil*

"Religion is not asking. It is a longing of the soul." *Gandhi*

"Running away from the object that we fear, only to realize a sweet surrender." *David P. Chaltas*

"Safe in the hallowed quiets of the past." *Lowell*

"Satan watches for those vessels that sail without a convoy." *George Swmnock*

"See in what peace a Christian can die." *Joseph Addison's last words*

"Seeing death as the end of life is like seeing the horizon as the end of the ocean." *David Searls*

"Since the day of my birth, my death began its walk. It is walking toward me, without hurrying." *Jean Cocteau*

"Sleep, those little slices of Death. How I loathe them." *Edgar Allen Poe*

"Someday I'll be a weather-beaten skull resting on a grass pillow, serenaded by a stray bird or two. Kings and commoners end up the same, no more enduring than last night's dream." *Ryokan*

"Some men are alive simply because it is against the law to kill them." *Ed Howe*

"Some people are so afraid to die that they never begin to live." *Henry Van Dyke*

"Strength is born in the deep silence of long-suffering hearts, not arid joy." *Hermans*

"Strike the tent." *General Robert E. Lee's last words*

"Suicide would be my way of telling God I quit." *Tom Kleffman*

"Tears are often the telescope by which men see far into heaven." *H.W. Beecher*

"Tears are the prayer-beads of all of us, men and women, because they arise from a fullness of the heart." *Edward Hays in Pray All Ways*

"Tears from the depths of some divine despair rise in the heart and gather to the eyes." *Alfred Lord Tennyson*

"Tell me not, in mournful numbers, life is but an empty dream! For the soul is dead that slumbers, and things are not what they seem. Life is real! Life is earnest! And the grave is not its goal. Dust thou art, to dust returnest, was not spoken of the soul." *Henry Wadsworth Longfellow*

"Tender is the touch of death for one so prepared." *Dave P. Chaltas*

"That awful yawn which sleep can not abate." *Lord Byron*

"That's all folks!" *Mel Blanc's tombstone epitaph*

"The best way to get to heaven is to take it with you." *Henry Drummond*

"The best things in life are nearest: Breath in your nostrils, light in your eyes, flowers at your feet, duties at your hand, the path of right just before you. Then do not grasp at the stars, but do life's plain, common work as it comes, certain that daily duties and daily bread are the sweetest things in life." *Robert Louis Stevenson*

"The bitterest tears shed over graves are for words left unsaid and deeds left undone." *Harriet Beecher Stowe*

"The call of death is a call of love. Death can be sweet if we accept it in the affirmative, if we accept it as one of the great eternal forms of life and transformation." *Hermann Hess*

"The clouds that gather round the setting sun, do take a sober coloring from an eye, that kept watch o'er man's mortality." *William Wordsworth*

"The cross leads generations on." *Shelley*

"The cycle of grief has its own timetable. Until that cycle is honored and completed we are moving along life's path with an anchor down." *Ann Linnea in Deep Water Passage*

"The day the Lord created hope was probably the same day he created spring." *Bern Williams*

"The day which we fear as our last is but the birthday of eternity." *Seneca*

"The deadliest of all sins is the mutilation of a child's spirit." *Erikson*

"The death of someone we know always reminds us that we are still alive-perhaps for some purpose which we ought to reexamine." *Mignon McLaughlin, the Neurotic's Notebook, 1960*

"The difficulty, my friends, is not in avoiding death, but in avoiding unrighteousness; for that runs faster than death." *Socrates*

"The dumber people think you are, the more surprised they're going to be when you kill them." *William Clayton*

"The end and the reward of toil is rest." *James Beattie*

"The fear of death follows from the fear of life. A man who lives fully is prepared to die at anytime." *Mark Twain*

"The fear of death is more to be dreaded than death itself." *Publilius Syrus*

"The fear of death keeps us from living, not from dying." *Paul C. Roud*

"The fear of death keeps us guarded from the joy of living, until we embrace the truth of God's love." *David P. Chaltas*

"The fear of death often proves mortal, and sets people on methods to save their lives, which infallibly destroy them." *Joseph Addison*

"The first breath is the beginning of death." *Thomas Fuller*

"The future belongs to those who believe in the beauty of their dreams." *Eleanor Roosevelt*

"The goal of life is death." *Sigmund Freud*

"The great Easter truth is not that we are to live newly after death, that is not the great thing, but that… we are to, and may, live nobly now because we are to live forever." *Phillips Brooks*

"The great use of life is to spend it for something that will outlast it." *William James*

"The graveyards are full of indispensable men." *Charles de Gaulle*

"The heart of him who truly loves is a paradise on earth." *Lamennais*

"The heart of man is restless until it finds its rest in Thee." *St. Augustine*

"The human heart feels things the eyes cannot see, and knows what the mind cannot." *Robert Vallett*

"The goal of all life is death." *Freud*

"The idea is to die young as late as possible." *Ashley Montagu*

"The key to the question of death unlocks the door to life." *Unknown*

"The last to be overcome is death, and the knowledge of life is the knowledge of death." *Edgar Cayce*

"The life we now live in is not the only one; what we call death is not an eternal sleep; the grave is not an everlasting prison, but the gate to an endless Life beyond." *General John B. Gordon*

"The lot of man – to suffer and to die." *Alexander Pope*

"The most beautiful thing we can experience is the mysterious. It is the source of all true art and science." *Albert Einstein*

"The most bitterest tears shed over graves are for words left unsaid and deeds left undone." *Unknown*

"The mystery of love is greater than the mystery of death." *Unknown*

"The only people helped by the death tax are lawyers, accountants, and IRS agents." *Rep. Bob Schaffer, R-Colorado*

"The purpose of life is a life of purpose." *Robert Byrne*

"The purpose of life is to matter-to count, to stand for something, to have it make some difference that we lived at all." *Leo Rosten*

"To teach men how to live without certainty and yet without being paralyzed by hesitation is the lesson of learning acceptance." *Anonymous*

"The question is not whether we will die, but how we will live." *Joan Borysenko*

"The only religious way to think of death is as a part and parcel of life; to regain it, with the understanding and the emotions, as the inviolable condition of life." *Thomas Mann*

"The only thing you take with you when you're gone is what you leave behind." *John Alliston*

"The silence that guards the tomb does not reveal God's secret in the obscurity of the coffin, and the rustling of the branches whose roots suck the body's elements do not tell the mysteries of the grave, by the agonized sighs of my heart announce to the living the drama which love, beauty, and death have performed.' *Kahlil Gibran*

"The soul that suffers is stronger than the soul that rejoices." *E. Shephard*

"The state of your life is nothing more than a reflection of your state of mind." *Dr. Wayne W. Dyer*

"The tragedy of life is not that it ends so soon, but that we wait so long to begin it."*W.M. Lewis*

"The thought of death does not frighten me, it merely reminds me to live, it reminds me to hug my children, it reminds me to tell my 81 year old father 'I love you!' it reminds me to smile and speak kind words to people I meet and people I know, it reminds me to do these things today, not tomorrow, for tomorrow will never come, but death surely will." *Wilma Riddle*

"The valley we call Death, Isn't really that different from much of the rest of the desert West. It's just a little deeper, a little hotter and a little drier. What sets it apart more than anything else is the mind's eye." *Richard E. Lingenfelter*

"The wailing of the newborn infant is mingled with the dirge for the dead." *Lucretius*

"The world is the mirror of myself dying." *Henry Miller*

"There are only two ways to live your life. One is as though nothing is a miracle. The other is as though everything is a miracle." *Albert Einstein*

"There are so many little silent dyings that it doesn't matter which of them is death." *Kenneth Patchen*

"There are worse things in life than dying. Have you ever spent an evening with an insurance salesman?" *Woody Allen*

"There is a sweet job that comes to us through sorrow." *Spurgeon*

"There is always death and taxes; however, death doesn't get worse every year." *Unknown*

"There is not a right or wrong way to grieve." *Unknown*

"There is dignity in dying that doctors should not dare to deny." *Unknown*

"There is no cure for birth and death save to enjoy the interval." *George Santayana*

"There is not death! What seems so is transition; this life of mortal breath is but a suburb of the life Elysian, Whose portal we call Death." *Henry W. Longfellow*

"There is no goal better than this one: to know as you lie on your deathbed that you lived life, and you did whatever made you happy." *Steve Chandler*

"There is nothing certain in a man's life except this: That he must lose it." *Aeschylus, Agamemnon*

"There is no goal better than this one: to know as you lie on your deathbed that you lived your true life, and you did whatever made you happy." *Steve Chandler*

"There is nothing which at once affects a man so much and so little as his own death." *Samuel Butler*

"There never was night that had no morn." *D. M. N. Craik*

"There will always be death and taxes; however, death doesn't get worse every year." *Unknown*

"Therefore, just as sin entered the world through one man, and death through sin, and in this way death came to all men, because all sinned."
Romans 5

"They shall not grow old, as we that are left grow old. Age shall not weary them, nor the years condemn. At the going down of the sun, and in the morning, we shall remember them." *Laurence Binyen, "For the Fallen"*

"Think not disdainfully of death, but look on with favor, for even death is one of the things that nature wills." *Marcus Aurelius Antoninus*

"This existence of ours is as transient as autumn clouds. To watch the birth and death of beings is like looking at the movements of a dance. A lifetime is a flash of lightning in the sky, rushing by like a torrent down a steep mountain." *Buddha (B.C.E. 568-488)*

"This suspense is killing me. I hope it lasts." *Willy Wonka*

"Those who cried the loudest at their moment of death were those who were found to have never really lived at all." *Kubler Ross*

"Tis true,' tis certain; and though dead retains, part of himself: the immortal mind remains." *Alexander Pope*

"Till the master of all good workmen shall set us to work anew." *Kipling*

"Time flies, death urges, knells call, Heaven invites, Hell threatens." *Edward Young*

"Tis very certain the desire of life prolongs it." *Lord Byron*

"To be idle is a short road to death and to be diligent is the way of life; foolish people are idle, wise people are diligent." *Buddha*

"To die proudly when it is no longer possible to live proudly. Death of one's own free choice, death at the proper time, with a clear head and with joyfulness, consummated in the midst of children and witnesses: so that an actual leave-taking is possible while he who is leaving is still there." *Friedrich Nietzsche*

"To everything there is a season, and a time to every purpose under the heaven. A time to be born, and a time to die. A time to plant, and a time to pluck up that which is planted. A time to kill, and a time to heal. A time to break down, and a time to build up. A time to weep, and a time to laugh. A time to mourn, and a time to dance. A time to cast away stones, and a time to gather stones together. A time to embrace, and a time to refrain from embracing. A time to get, and a time to lose. A time to keep, and a time to cast away. A time to rend and a time to sew. A time to keep silence, and a time to speak, a time to love and a time to hate; a time of war, and a time of peace." *Ecc 3: 1-8*

"To himself, everyone is immortal. He may know that he is going to die, but he can never known that he is dead." *Samuel Butler*

"To infinite, ever present love, all is love, and there is no error, no sin, sickness, or death." *Mary Baker Eddy*

"To the psychotherapist an old man who cannot bid farewell to life appears as feeble and sickly as a young man who is unable to embrace it." *C. G. Jung*

"To the well organized mind, death is but the next great adventure." *Albus Cumbledore*

"To the world you might be one person, but to one person you might be world." *Unknown*

"Tomorrow, and tomorrow, and tomorrow creeps in this petty pace from day to day so the last syllable of recorded time, and all our yesterdays have lighted fools the way to the dusty death. Out, out, brief candle! Life is but a walking shadow, a poor player that struts and frets his hour upon the stage and then is heard no more. It is a tale told by an idiot, full of sound, signifying nothing." *Shakespeare, Macbeth*

"Too busy with the crowded hour to fear to live or die." *Ralph Waldo Emerson*

"Troubles are often the tools which God fashions us for better things." *Henry Ward Beecher*

"Truth sits upon the lips of dying men." *Matthew Arnold*

"Until the day break, and the shadows flee away." *Cant.li:17*

"Until the day of his death, no man can be sure of his courage." *Jean Anouilh*

(Widows Weeds at the Hunley Funeral, April 17, 2004)

"We all labor against our own cure, for death is the cure for all diseases." *Unknown*

"We are afraid to live, but scared to die." *Inderpal Bahra*

"We are all dead men on leave." *Eugene Levine*

"We are born with two incurable diseases, life, from which we die, and hope, which says maybe death isn't the end." *Andrew Greeley*

"We are here to laugh at the odds and live our lives so well that Death will tremble to take us." *Charles Bukowski*

"We are ignorant of the Beyond because this ignorance is the condition of our own life. Just as ice cannot know fire except by melting and vanishing." *Jules Renard*

"We are not human beings having a spiritual experience. We are spiritual beings having a human experience." *Dr. Wayne Dyer*

"We can not banish danger, but we can banish fears. We must not demean life by standing in awe of death." *David Sarnoff*

"We cast away priceless time in dreams, born of imagination, fed upon illusion and put to death by reality." *Judy Garland*

"We know that we have passed from death to life, because we love our brothers. Anyone who does not love remains in death." *1 John 3*

'We must love one another or die." *Jack Lemmon*

"We owe a deep dept of gratitude to Adam, the first great benefactor of the human race: he brought death into the world." *Mark Twain*

"We say that the hour of death cannot be forecast, but when we say this we imagine that hour as placed in an obscure and distant future. It never occurs to us that it has any connection with the day already begun or that death could arrive this same afternoon, this afternoon which is so certain and which has every hour filled in advance." *Marcel Proust*

"We shall draw from the heart of suffering itself the means of inspiration and survival." *Winston Churchill*

"We sometimes congratulate ourselves at the moment of waking from a troubled dream...It may be so at the moment of death." *Nathaniel Hawthorne*

"We trust to her a place is given among the saints with Christ in Heaven." *Epitaph*

"We understand death for the first time when he puts his hand upon one whom we love." *Madame de Stael*

"We were born to die and we die to live. As seedlings of God, we barely blossom on earth; we fully flower in heaven." *Russell M. Nelson*

"We will not all sleep, but we will all be changed in a flash, in the twinkling of an eye, at the last trumpet. For the trumpet will sound, the dead will be raised imperishable, and we will be changed. For the perishable must clothe itself with the imperishable, and the mortal with immortality. When the perishable has been clothed with the imperishable, and the mortal with immortality, then the saying that is written will come true: 'Death has been swallowed up in victory.' Where, O death, is your victory? Where, O death, is your sting?' The sting of death is sin, and the power of sin is the law. The last enemy to be destroyed is death." *1 Corinthians 15*

"What is death but a passage to life?" *Travis M. Farnsworth*

"What is your life? You are a mist that appears for a little while and then vanishes." *James 4*

"What seems to us but dim funeral tapers may be heaven's distant lamps." *Longfellow*

"What then remains but that we still should cry, for being born, and, being born, to die." *Francis Bacon*

"What we call the beginning is often the end. And to make an end is to make a beginning. The end is where we start from." *T. S. Eliot*

"What we commonly call death does not destroy the body, it only causes a separation of spirit and body." *Brigham Young*

"What we have done for ourselves alone dies with us; what we have done for others and the world remains and is immortal." *Albert Pike*

"Whatever you do in life and love is forever etched in the hearts of those that it affects." *Unknown*

"When I look back on all these worries, I remember the story of the old man who said on his deathbed that he had had a lot of trouble in his life, most of which had never happened." *Winston Churchill*

"When I stand before God at the end of my life, I would hope that I would not have a single bit of talent left and I could say, " I used everything you gave me." *Erma Bombeck*

"When I think of death, I think of life and smile." *David P. Chaltas*

"When one man dies, one chapter is not torn out of the book, but translated into a better language." *John Donne*

"When tears come, I breathe deeply and rest. I know I am swimming in a hallowed stream where many have gone before. I am not alone, crazy, or having a nervous breakdown… My heart is at work. My soul is awake." *Mary Margaret Funk in Thoughts Matter*

"When we attempt to imagine death, we perceive ourselves as spectators." *Sigmund Freud*

"When we die and we go to heaven, and we meet our Maker, our Maker is not going to say to us, why didn't you become a messiah? Why didn't you discover the cure for such and such? The only thing we're going to be asked at that precious moment is

why didn't you become you." *Wiesel in* <u>*Souls on*</u>
<u>*Fire*</u>

"When you were born you cried and the world
rejoiced, so you must live your life in such a
manner that when you die the world cries but you
rejoice." *Unknown*

"When the heart weeps for what it has lost, the soul
laughs for what it has found." *Sufi Aphorism*

"When the body sinks into death, the essence of
man is revealed. Man is a knot, a web, a mesh into
which relationships are tied. Only those
relationships matter. The body is an old crock that
nobody will miss. I have never known a man to
think of himself when dying. Never." *Antoine de
Saint-Exupery*

"When you reach for the stars, you may not quite
get them, but you won't come up with a handful of
mud either." *Leo Burnett*

"Where my heart leads me I can safely go." *Milay*

"Where there is much light, the shadows are
deepest." *Goethe*

"Where there is sorrow there is holy ground." *Wilde*

"While I thought I was learning how to live, I have
been learning how to die." *Leonardo de Vinci*

"While we are mourning the loss of our friend,
others are rejoicing to meet him behind the veil."
John Taylor

"Who dies in youth and vigour, dies the best."
Alexander Pope

"Whither thou goest, I will go." *Ruth 1:16*

"Years, following years, steal something every day; at last they steal us from ourselves away." *Horace*

"You are the dreamer and the dream." *Unknown*

"You can't do anything about the length of your life, but you can do something about its width and depth." *Shira Tehrani*

"You do not know what will happen tomorrow."
James 4:14

"You do not understand even life. How can you understand death?" *Confucius*

"You live on earth only for a few short years which you call an incarnation, and then you leave your body as an outworn dress and go for the refreshment to your true home in the spirit" *White Eagle*

"You see sir; death is an intellectual matter, but dying is pure pain." *John Steinbeck*

"You want to live – but do you know how to live? You are scared of dying and, tell me, is the kind of life you lead really any different from being dead?" *Seneca*

REFLECTIONS OF THE PASSING

"Personal Narratives of the Passing"

Reflections of Aunt Ellie

Good Morning My Dear Cousins,

I know this day weighs heavily upon your heart but know that not only my prayers are with you but those of my prayer partners across this nation. I cannot fathom the loss of dear Aunt Ellie for she was unchanging in my eyes. But God has a new rose within His garden and she is at rest with all those she loved. Your loss is great but heaven's gain is greater and know this: "He will not leave us as orphans, He will come to you." "God also promises us that He will not place upon us more than we can bear." Still after 8 years, I have pains of longing for my mother, but mixed with my sadness is pure joy for her; for I know she is resting under the shade of the trees and on occasion I can hear her laughing with her loved ones once again, and it is enough to sustain me. Her spirit has been released. No more pain, no sorrow, no crying; only the joy that passeth our understanding of being with our Savior and family. Now there is another dear angel playing and singing, with no regrets. Rest assured that when we came into this world, a loving God was there releasing us to walk upon this world and He is waiting at the end of our journey on earth to receive us with open arms. We serve a merciful loving God and your little mother is home now, where one day we all shall also be. For that is His divine plan.

I have Saturday School this day but am trying to get someone to come in and take my place this afternoon so I can come to the funeral. If I can't make it in person, please believe that my heart will be there and I will go by Lexington Cemetery to pay my respects. Every time I come to Lexington I drop by your father and brother's gravesite. It is so peaceful there. With a deepened sense of sadness softened with the knowledge of His Love.

I found these sayings helpful to me when mom passed on...

"Be strong and of good courage, fear not, nor be afraid...for the Lord thy God he it is that doth go with thee; he will not fail thee, nor forsake thee." Deuteronomy

"Death, in its silent, sure march is fast gathering those whom I have longest loved, so that when he shall knock at my door, I will more willingly follow." R. E. Lee

"It is God's love for us that sends us on our journey and it is our love for God that allows us to return to God's loving arms again." David Goines

I shall remain your loving cousin, D. P. Chaltas

The Passing of Ms. Jane Dixon
"The Realization"

The realization came crashing down upon my spirit like a gigantic Tsunami. For this morning I received a phone call stating that my dear friend had passed through that turbid vale and now rests with her ancestors. You see she was my friend; my friend Mike's wife, and we all had grown up together. One thing was always consistent: Janie would always be there. She was so intelligent, possessing the voice of an angel and carrying herself in all things like a lady. The realization shattered the myth that tomorrow I could express my gratitude for all the meals that she cooked for me and all the times we sat around singing, playing music, and laughing. The realization that her laugh would not always permeate the walls of her house had never entered the perimeters of my mind. I never fathomed the realization of not being able to just drop by their home, sit on the porch sharing childhood days, our days on the reservation, our days hanging around C. B. Caudill's store, and our days of dreams and delight. My realization that I had taken for granted a gift from God by not visiting those I love like I should due to my 'busy self-imposed' world of work came crashing down upon my being with such a force that I was unable to think of anything other than the loss.

I remember her positive nature and how she always saw the Christian in a sea full of sinners. I remember her love for life and genuineness of spirit. There were literally thousands of miles we traveled together as we ventured forth into the great unknown together. Was it not only yesterday that we strolled within the confines of Blue Canyon and gazed at the wonder of God's creations, or watched with amazement the sites of an Arizona sunset? This wondrous lady, with such a mastery of the English language, gave me so many gifts of life that I shall always cherish. A saying comes to my mind as I reflect upon the realization. No the saying IS the realization! It simply states, and yet so powerfully declares, what I feel I have failed to do. "Treasure each other in the recognition that you will not always have one another."

Ms. Janie, I thank you for all you gave, not only to me but also to those that your life has touched. I now realize the significance of you in my life and know that I have been blessed with precious memories that will linger within my mind forever and a day. As your spirit passeth by, I shall mourn your loss beside my brother Mike and niece Nik, but rejoice with the knowledge that you rest in a new bed of roses and are walking with the angels. Knowing that I shall see her once again and that I too will someday wade into the water to reach the other shore soothes the ache within my soul. The realization of blessed assurance reassures my doubt.

"But in the night of death hope sees a star, and listening love can hear the rustle of a wing."
Ingeresoll

"Death is nothing else but going home to God, the bond of love will be unbroken for all eternity."
Mother Teresa

"Death, in its silent, sure march is fast gathering those whom I have longest loved, so that when he shall knock at my door, I will more willingly follow." *R. E. Lee*

"It is God's love for us that sends us on our journey and it is our love for God that allows us to return to God's loving arms again." *David Goines*

A Tribute to Jane

The following is a letter of love from Mike, her husband, for Janie and is a tribute of never ending love shining through the evening mist. The wrens pay tribute to a lady of legend.

"Sunday was our 38th wedding anniversary. I painted two small birds for Jane and sat them on the chest where she could see them. She smiled through the pain.

"This morning, I noticed that the wren out the back window that sings at daybreak too loudly for its little body was silent. As I made the coffee, the Kentucky mountain mist rose up Stillhouse Branch over by the store and the little house where we lived when we were first married. The sun came out and touched the tiptop of the mountain and then it quickly became cloudy. By late morning, the sky gradually cleared and the most beautiful Arizona blue that Janie so loved filled the day. Finally, as the shadows crept up from the North Fork and climbed the hill out the back window, and just as the last glimmer of light faded from the blue-green sky, Jane went so easily and so gently.

"Nikki and I were by her side, and her Aunt Charlie. We held her hands, talked about love, and gave her permission to go when she was ready. It really was without any suffering. We are so glad that it happened that way and so glad that the suffering has ended. There are no answers here and nothing to be learned, but maybe love always shines above it all and this gives us the chance to see it." Michael

Reflections of Michael
September 1, 1991-November 13, 2003
David Chaltas

In today's busy bustling world, sometimes we forget to stop and count the many blessings that have been given unto us. We all are guilty of getting caught up into society's time game as we misappropriate our energies into things that allow us to survive without really living. My great wake up call came about three and a half years ago when a little third grader entered my life. He was a small child with dancing eyes and a smile that brought out the motherly or fatherly instinct in adults. He was a fast talker who crammed a thousand words into a minute and his mind raced with ideas. He was a child born with a heart on the wrong side and only possessed two chambers therefore requiring home bound instruction. And I was the one selected in "his" interview of teachers.

I knew from the first that I was in for a challenge. His mind was so much quicker than mine as he jumped from one concept to the next, often to my dismay and displeasure. He introduced me to the most unusual world of Pokemon and Digiman and could tell every aspect of their origins and existence again to my dismay. For I held the grand idea that I must teach him the rudiments of education when all along he was teaching me the essentials of life. It was a battle at times to work on math and often I would go away frustrated in that I saw the brilliance of the child yet could not even open the door of motivation to reach him. He refused to read and hated spelling yet something was there far above those basic concepts that a teacher holds so dear within the confines of the heart.

He was always delighted to see me but there were times that he did not want to stay due to being too tired to work. Of course I saw this as an excuse and in my efforts to make him a normal little boy in a world, I would sometimes forget his hidden illness and chastise him for not wanting to stay. Allene Wright, his devoted grandmother would also become upset but we would yield the ground to him when he would say, "I won't be needing to read or write where I'm going."

I remember the first time I visited him when he became sick and was hospitalized. I went in the room expecting to see the boy that possessed so much passion for life sitting up in his bed talking and asking a hundred questions at once but instead to my dismay I saw a sickly child that shocked me into his world. After the visit I went home and started thinking in terms of his needs and how I could offer a holistic education inclusive of counseling. The next days visit found Mikie sitting up, playing his Play Station and so full of life that I noted it as a miracle and vowed to do my share in his recovery.

When he was able to return to "evening school" as he called it, I gathered the books that I chose and symbolically discarded them. I actively listened to what he wanted to learn and began developing a curriculum. Then it dawned upon my being to use his strengths; tap into that grand imagination that he possessed. On our next encounter I talked about my writings and read to him a couple of stories that I had written and asked him would he be interested in creating a book. He went for it hook, line and sinker! I found myself engulfed with ideas that he presented and then he stated, "I've always wanted to write about a crystal dragon" and the saga began. He would tell me so much information that I would have to halt his creative juices to catch up and when I questioned him about the direction of the story, he'd say, "Trust me on this, I know what I'm doing and where I'm going" and he always did. I would have him "proof" the wording and select the spelling words from his story. He would work diligently in this world of fantasy where he possessed the ability to run, jump, play and defend the goodness of his world. We both became absorbed to the point that we couldn't wait until the next chapter and then the next book. We talked of selling the book and that's where the money math came into play. We started counting the words and deciding on how many per page we could get with certain font. We began exploring artistic expressions and decided to use his talents in the book. I would quiz him on concepts and read to him stories to entice his imaginings. He grew but I grew more.

I recall the year in which I had decided not to teach Michael. It was due to my own health related problems. Well Michael would not have any of it. The regular homebound teacher went out and Michael threw a pure tantrum. He refused to even consider having anyone else. Central Office called but I held my ground firmly. The grandmother asked me to reconsider but it was when Michael called and stated he would work on those old boring books if I would be his teacher that my heart mended. Well, we didn't open those old "boring books" but we continued doing things our way and loving the concepts that we discovered through "Blood and Guts" science, "Young Astronaut" material and surfing the waves of his genius. When regular school had ended and the time approached for him to appear I found myself watching the clock and saying, "Here's Michael" in the tradition of Ed McMahon to my constituents upon his arrival. Our bond grew.

We had always played the game of "find Michael" before class began as he hid under my desk or somewhere in the confines of my building. I would pretend to be upset when I could not find him but all the while yielding to his smile that permeated the room with its radiance. He would apologize and begin his "Bob Cratchet" chores, as he used to call them. But I found those moments fleeting towards the end. He knew and he would often say to his grandmother and me that he "Wouldn't need to read or write soon." With usual adulthood denial that he was swiftly shrinking we insisted on him putting forth an effort.

Towards the latter part of the last year, he started slipping and could no longer do the things that brought him the joy of childhood. He tired easily and could not walk far without taking "a breather." He would have to hesitate and rest when walking but always refusing to use his wheelchair. He would turn blue to a purple hue and I would have to monitor his color as well as his heart rate. He began making frequent retreats to the hospital for longer lengths of time. But never once did he complain about his condition. He seemed to be more worried about my obvious concern and would reassure me that it was OK.

He had been on a donor list for an extended period of time but he was too frail to withstand the operation. But out of desperation and his rapid deterioration the time came in which his visit to University of Kentucky was not enough to revive him. This time he was immediately taken again to the University of Pittsburgh's Children's Hospital and this time placed on a priority list for a new heart.

I recall that day when I called him at 9:13 and he cracked a couple of jokes. In retrospect, I do believe the jokes were meant to ease my mind. I told him I would see him in Pittsburgh and he said, "Take your time" instead of the usual "OK" or "Hurry down."

The flight left around 9:30 that morning and he was sitting up entertaining the EMTs and his grandmother. He was looking out his window with an air of contentment when he looked over at his grandmother and stated, "God has a greater purpose for me" and then smiled. She took his picture and in a couple of minutes he said, "I have a headache" and collapsed. The EMTs gallantly worked with him for over two hours as they flew him to the Children's Hospital. His body lingered but he had departed to a better world and 2 days later they released his body from this earthly bondage as a shooting star raced across the heavens on its way home.

The following notice was put on our list server to inform people nation wide that had prayed for this child that he had a new heart. I entitled it Reflections of Michael. I offer it to you in tribute to this young hero that has found the desire of his heart; to run and play baseball and ride upon the back of a crystal dragon.

It is with great sadness and the deepest sense of sorrow that I must report the loss of our gallant little warrior. He loved listening to the tales of yesteryear and was so proud of his own ancestry. We would talk for hours about the Great Conflict and he would always interject a dragon or magical spell that could have won the battle for the boys in gray. Michael Alan Wright succumbed to the will of our Lord on November 13, 2003, at 7:00 P.M while at the University of Pittsburgh Children's Hospital. He was 12 years, 2 months and 11 days of age at the time of his passing. His little heart could not sustain his 12-year-old body and he was too weak to undergo the desperately needed transplant. His final battle began while being flown from UK to Pittsburgh. The family wishes to convey their heartfelt gratitude by the national outpouring of prayers for this wonderful little boy.

As his homebound instructor for over 4 years, I too offer my gratitude and humble myself at the foot of our Lord in submission to His Divine Will. We just completed the work on his book entitled; "The Crystal Dragon" and I shall do all I can to get it published, as he so desired. We must accept that our loving God heard the petition of the people but needed a beautiful flower for his garden. Though young Michael walks the earth no more, I know that he is running upon the wind in the Fields of Glory with the joy & freedom that eluded him while he was amongst us. Please pray that the Comforter will surround those left behind and shield them from the ravages of their loss.

When asked by the family to write a poem about Michael, I wondered what I could say to capture the essence of this special child? Should I tell of our many talks about dragons or how excited he got when I brought him a gift? Should I share the time he beat me in four moves in chess or the time I made him cry when I talked about death? Should I tell of his warrior's heart and how he never complained to me about how bad he felt or how he would ask me if his fingers were turning blue? Could I mention how generous he was and if he had money for a snack, he would always offer to buy me something first?

Should I explain that he had such a vivid imagination that I was often amazed as to his intelligence? Do I speak of his innocence and great sense of humor? Should I tell of the numerous times he would hide from me and whenever I "gave up" the search for him he would come out in childhood delight? Do I state that he was always so well mannered, so likeable and easy going with his friends? Should I talk of his trip to Rupp Arena on June 9, 2001, when he met the Backstreet Boys and how he glowed whenever he talked of that wondrous day in June?

Do I share the time when we walked to the Pet Store and he had to stop three times to catch his breath and when he saw the worried look on my brow he attempted to reassure me? Would they want to hear of how he loved to listen to me read about dragons, the Jack Tales and stories of the War Between the States and then afterwards answer every question with such in-depth understanding? Would they understand <u>his</u> sense of pride when he saw his teacher wearing the uniform that made him look like General Lee? Is this the time that I reflect upon our last conversation prior to the flight to Pittsburgh when at 9:15 I called him and expressed how "jealous" I was that he was going to fly all the way to Pittsburgh and I had to drive and immediately yet humorously he replied, "Wanna trade places?" Should I dare say that he would get upset when trying to read and at times I would also become upset due to his lack of effort? What should I say that would offer comfort? Where are the words? Then by divine revelation it came upon my being that I need not say anything about him, for those who truly knew him already understood the greatness of this child. I need only say that I loved him as a son and will sorely miss his dancing eyes, quick wit, and wondrous spirit that I know now entertains our gracious loving God. To me he seems a hero.

The poem that I entitled "Little Sparrow" brings to play Michael's dreams of running and playing like other children. It shares his world of imaginings: a world where he could do magical things and possessed those abilities that he longed for. It talks of his undampened spirit that lit up the room with its radiance. It expresses the faith in the promise of a better tomorrow and acknowledges that as the sparrow received new wings, Michael has a new heart; and a star shoots to the heavens to proclaim another angel is coming home.

I do remain your humbled servant,

The Old General

"Little Sparrow"
November 14, 2003

His little wings were broken:
He could not learn to fly.
His fears were never spoken.
You never heard him cry.

He had a Crystal Dragon
That shielded him from harm.
And with its huge tail wagging,
It kept him safe and warm.

The dragon granted wishes.
He rode upon its back.
It showered him with kisses
And placed them in his pack.

The tiny little sparrow
Soon learned to walk the wind.

Though facing many perils,
He'd always seem to win.

His spirit was uplifting.
His smile would hide the sun!
But slowly he was drifting.
His journey had begun.

How swiftly he has faded!
Oh, how we loathe to mourn.
But his wings were created:
Another angel's born!

So go fly little sparrow!
Your wings had been restored.
Go fly straight and narrow
While dancing for the Lord.

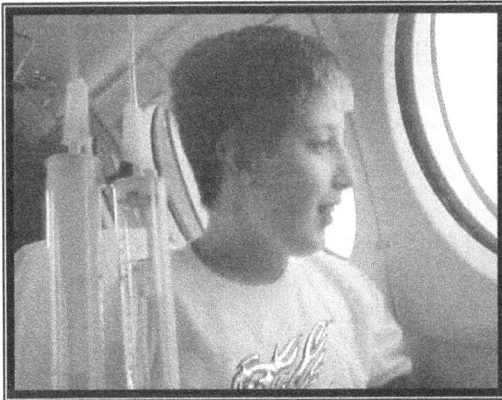

"He has his Wings!"

"By faith we are conquerors of all things and hold
within our hearts a promise of tomorrow."
Dave Chaltas

The Smell of Roses and Promises Kept
Shawana Slone

Eventually in our lifetime we will face the death of a loved one that we have felt we could never bear the pain of losing. How we deal with that loss is up to us. We must accept the fact that dying is a part of living. We can run and hide from the fact or we can choose to stand close by and savor the precious time we have left with those we love. As being raised as an only child, my hardest loss was that of my mother. That loss became a turning point in my life. To an extent it has been my eye-opener not only on death but what it can be. This is my story.

I sat alone with my dying, sixty-two year old, mother throughout the night on April 27, 2003, watching her and holding her hand for I knew this would be my last chance to do this. This was the night I would keep my promise. My mind scanned memories of the many happy moments I had spent with her. She had always been my one constant. She had more or less raised me by herself. She had labored long hours as a waitress/cook to provide a roof over my head. No matter how hard times got she always managed to clothe, feed, and send me to school. She had always been my comfort and encouragement. Life had always been her and me against the world so to speak.

When the doctors had told her that she had developed a tumor in her left lung that January, it was devastating. Shock is the only way it could be described. Momma had been doing her all her normal summer routines that year. She worked on her household chores. She had spent many hours working in her flowerbeds and her small rose beds. Roses had always been her favorite flower, she would spend time every day pulling the weeds from around them talking to her "babies". How she loved her roses. I loved to watch her touch their tender petals so lovingly before she would smell their perfume. She had always been so active and full of life. This news seemed to drain the life out her. I watched over the next four months as the woman I had always admired for her strength and her will to survive weaken and become so frail. Sometimes she looked as fragile as her roses. She made her decision to not opt for chemo or radiation treatments to shrink the tumor so the doctors could perform surgery. Although this broke my heart, I tried hard to accept it; however, I wanted to deny the fact I was losing her with everything in my being. Now looking back I know I was only being so selfish to want to keep her here longer than she desired to stay. I kept hoping it was only a bad dream and sooner or later I would awake and find everything back to normal. I watched as she signed the advanced directive to not be resuscitated with a lump the size of a fist in my throat. She looked at me and said, " Promise me you will not let them bring me back, once I'm gone make them let me rest." I could only nod my head and reply, "If that is what you want, momma. I promise." Promise number one. I listened to the plans she wanted carried forward for her funeral wondering why is this happening now? I knew in my heart that she was trying to help me through this; she wanted to make it as easy as she could, but each thing she prepared was a reminder of what was going to happen soon.

About a month before she died, Momma told of a fear she had. Her fear was dying alone. She asked if I would be with her. The sadness I felt at that moment was overpowering. I choked back my tears and promised her I would try my best to be there with her and help her pass over to a new life. Promise number two. I wanted so desperately to ease her mind so I kept my own fear hidden from her as well as everyone else. My fear was I didn't think I would be able to keep this promise. In my mind I kept thinking, "I can't do this. I can't face this. I refuse to accept she is leaving me so soon. I can't watch her take her last breath." I carried this burden hidden in my heart alone. I felt as if I told someone they would tell her or judge me in some way or another.

The months passed so quickly it was if time had been set in fast forward. Her last week here seems almost as a dream I walked through blindly. The family came and went throughout the days but the nights were mine. We spent them talking about things we had seen or done together. We laughed a lot and cried some too. It was if she wanted to relive her life with me sometimes. A few nights before she passed she looked at me and inquired, "Can you accept that I'm leaving?" This stunned me. I looked at her weary, blue eyes and said, "Honestly, Momma, I don't want to but I know I have to." Her reply was, "I don't want you to grieve over me. You have been a good daughter to me. You have brought me so much happiness. So don't grieve. Just remember that I love you. Promise me that." Promise number 3. Another promise I thought I would never be able to keep but I still promised just the same.

The morning of April 27th, I was informed she would not last much longer, probably only through the night. Family members begged and pleaded for me to go home and get some rest but the only thing in my mind was the promise I had made to stay with her. A voice from my conscience kicked in. It kept telling me, "She helped you enter this world, it's only fair for you to help her enter a new one." So I found a new strength, a force to drive me to keep this promise. The next morning of the 28th, I found myself setting beside her bedside with her hand in mine. Two nurses stayed in the room with us monitoring her condition. One told me it would not be long. Momma had turned her head toward me and it was if she was looking at me one last time waiting for me to speak to her. I took one hand and brushed back her hair and down her soft cheek. I said to her, "Momma, I'm here. I love you, and it's ok. You've been the best mommy in the world." She smiled, closed her eyes, and took her last breath. The nurse who had been standing beside me said, " She's gone. Do you want us to try and resuscitate her?" No sooner than the word no had left my mouth an odor so familiar to me filled the room. The scent of roses. It was not the odor of flower shop roses but the smell of momma's garden roses. I looked up at the nurses and said, "I smell roses. Can you smell them? Why do I smell roses?" They only shook their heads and shrugged their shoulders before they left the room.

As I walked out of the hospital that morning the scent of roses lingered with me. Outside the sky was a bright blue and a gentle breeze touched my face. It was spring momma's favorite time of year.

She had always said she wanted to die in the spring. My life was now changed yet my heart had a soulful peace within it. I had granted one of my promises made to my mother. I knew the roses I smelled were a sign for me to carry throughout my life, a sign that she knew I had done what was asked of me. It was her way of telling me she, my precious rose, was now a rose in her Master's bouquet.

Many people have asked me if the experience of watching my mother die has effected me in any way. To this I can only reply yes it has to a degree. The effect it has left me with has been great peace. I don't look at this experience as an ending. I view it as a simple change. My mother shall always be with me in my memories. She is not gone. She only exists in a different sense. I see her in me each time I look in the mirror. I see and hear her laughter in my child, and no doubt, I will see her in my grandchildren. One of the biggest changes is now I take the time to enjoy the scent of her garden roses for their aroma and beauty will always remind me of her love for me which helps me keep my second promise to her.

Personal Reflections

I did something this morning that I never thought I would really have to do. I went to a wake for a friend/ex-boyfriend. He wrecked a motorcycle and he never survived. I went this morning because I didn't expect a lot of people to be there but his mother was there. His brother showed up before I left. I not only dated him we were friends and used to hang out together. I hung out with his brother and cousins a lot too but I haven't seen him until

88

about 6-7 months ago. We talked briefly about unimportant things, mostly about dogs. He was raising dogs and selling them, making pretty good money. It was more like strangers talking than old friends. I really have been thinking a lot about that these last few days when I looked at him this morning. It was very hard to see him this way. He was always laughing and making jokes. To see his face pale and his lips bluish, it seemed so unreal for me. Here is this guy that once made me feel like a princess, that I could never do anything wrong laying there not breathing. I wondered why it was him? He never used drugs or drank. He always did what he thought was right. He had a wife and a baby six-months old. I think they were trying for another. His entire life was ahead of him and there he lay dead. It was hard for me to see him like that and when his mom told me she was glad I came there, that she always loved me, it was so painful that I could not contain myself. Once I came back home, I sat thinking that was the fourth funeral/wake that I went to this past year and how awful his family must feel. How it will be hard for them to go on with their lives because he played such a big part of it. All of us must face death but it feels so bad.

The Sky On a Clear Day
Amber K. Lewis

My mother got married young so it was no surprise to anyone what happened once her and my father was divorced. Her priorities went from being a mother to finding herself. During this "search", my siblings and I were left in the hands of my grandparents. They were hard working and finished raising their own five children many years earlier. They lived on a mountain in a place that I still believe today was one of the most beautiful places in the world. Up above their home was a beautiful mountainside full of trees and large rocks, which offered the best play area a kid could ever wish for. Running down the middle of this heavenly mountainside was a creek that my siblings and I would play in for hours until the sun rested so far behind the mountain that there was barely enough light to guide our way back home. The landscape in front of the house was just as magical. It offered an abundance of trees and even a large shed that served as the most perfect spot for games like hide and seek. I remember countless hours spent making mud pies on my grandparent's front porch looking out past the trees and shed to the world in front of me. It felt as if I could see forever and nothing was impossible.

My grandparents were even more wonderful than the environment in which they lived. They worked hard to instill in the family the ethics and values that made them the center of love and respect for who they were. Many afternoons was a Bible lesson at my Grandmother's kitchen table. While rabbits were bouncing through the yard, and the evening's supper was simmering on the stove, my beautiful Grandmother would sit across the table from us and read to us from her cherished worn Bible. She would give us words of peace and wisdom that she knew we would desperately need one day. She would tell us about Heaven and tears would come to her eyes as she spoke of one day going there and meeting Jesus and her own mother that she had missed for so many years.

They would get up early of a morning to work their huge garden. So early, in fact, sometimes I wondered if the birds even got up that early. If the garden didn't need to be tended, they would take us on long walks. We would follow the railroad tracks near the house and slowly we would walk taking in every beautiful thing around us. My grandfather with his walking cane and my grandmother with a container of water in one hand and my own hand in her other. No matter how tired they were, they always made sure to take us to the railroad bridge, which was my favorite spot. It was a one-mile walk from home but it was well worth the effort. We would stand in the middle of the bridge and look down at the mesmerizing river below us. My grandfather would stand and point out every amazing sound of Mother Nature dancing around us. Standing there with my grandparents, I felt the safest I had ever been. I was truly blessed.

A cold December morning at the age of twelve, my world came crashing down. I was awakened by strange sounds coming from the living room. It was December so I knew that no one would be getting ready to go to the garden. It was definitely too cold for an early morning walk. As I climbed out of my warm safe bed, I soon realized that something was terribly wrong. My heart pounded as I walked through the hall toward the living room. And to my absolute horror, I saw my grandmother lying on the couch having what turned out to be a stroke. Her eyes were closed and yet she was yelling incoherent words. She had awakened sometime in the morning unable to sleep. She was wearing her housecoat and shoes and the coffee brew was brewing in the kitchen. My grandfather had also awakened and now sat in a chair next to my grandmother holding her hand and not knowing what to do. As the ambulance drove off, I knew that they weren't just taking away my grandmother but taking away my safe beautiful world that had for years surrounded and blessed me. She lived for three days in the local hospital slipping in and out of consciousness until the strokes wore her tired body. It was misery living without her. The pain my heart felt hurt to an unbearable extent and seemed to stay there. I truly believed it would never go away.

My grandfather's health immediately started deteriorating. My mother attempted to do what was right and to take care of him. But there was no substitute for my grandmother. Without her, everything seemed to fall apart. Eventually, my grandfather ended up in a nursing home. His health and mental status reached a point where he needed more care than we could provide.

Being left to live in my grandparent's home with my siblings and my mother, I spent my teenage years in a slow downhill depression. I was surrounded by memories. Some beautiful and some horrible. I found solitude in visiting my grandfather. Some days he would know who I was and some days he wouldn't. Either way, my grandfather would look at me with the most amazing blue eyes I had ever seen. They were the color of the sky on a perfectly clear day. It would remind me of lying on the grass on a sunny morning staring up at the world above me while listening to my grandparent's till the garden. Looking in his eyes in that certain moment gave me a piece of the love and warmth that I desperately longed for.

At the age of seventeen, I could take pain no more. I took the ethics and values given to me by my grandparents and left the loneliness behind to start a new life. I got married and within a month, I found out I was pregnant. My grandfather always loved the laughter and free-spirited wonder that children brought. I knew that this baby would be a new chance of happiness to give him. For so long we had all lived pain and for the first time there was light at the end of the tunnel. I wanted my baby to sit in his lap and look up at the beautiful blue eyes that had always give me so much comfort. I was excited about having the chance for my child to meet him. I wanted to tell her stories about my childhood and share my grandfather with her. It was the one true blessing I knew that I could provide her.

Unfortunately, my grandfather didn't live long enough. He passed away before getting to see my baby. Again, I was devastated. I relived the pain anew. Over time, the pain became less severe and I looked forward to and planned my future with my husband and baby. But as the nine months of pregnancy came to an end, it saddened me at the thought of not having the chance to walk into my grandfather's room and see the look on his face as I showed him the new gift of joy in my life.

Upon her arrival, she was definitely more than I ever dreamed of. I never knew I could love something so much. But there was something else about her. Something that took my breath away as I looked down at the tiny miracle that cried in my arms. She had the most amazing blue eyes I had ever seen. It was like the color of the sky on a perfectly clear day. And in that moment, I was taken back to the place of love and warmth. The place I desperately longed to be. The place I was finally at yet again.

In Memory of Lola Bates Honeycutt
March 28, 1906-September 24, 2006
David Chaltas and Richard Brown

My Kepi and Me is a series honoring camp members and their ancestors. The purpose is to share their ancestor's history as well as the current son/daughter occupying the seat of honor. This month let us stand and offer a silent tribute to our real daughter, *Ms. Lola Bates Honeycutt.* Ms. Lola was born on March 28, 1906. She was the daughter of Captain Robert and Elizabeth Bentley Bates. Elizabeth Bentley Bates was the daughter of Lieutenant Aaron Rice and Darcus Hall Bates (1844-1918). Their union resulted in four children.

Aaron Rice Bentley was born in 1836 to Solomon and Mary Bentley. His brothers were Barrett and Benjamin Bentley. Both brothers served in the Confederate army with their younger brother, Aaron (Barrett had also served in Diamond's 10th KY Cavalry, Company E). Aaron Rice reportedly was six foot tall and had dark hair. He enlisted in the 13th KY on October 18, 1862. Aaron Rice Bentley had served in the 5th KY 'Orphan Brigade', Company F and was elected Lieutenant in Company H of the 13th Kentucky Cavalry. Union Home Guards wounded him (allegedly the notorious Clabe Jones) during a skirmish up Mason's Creek in Perry County, Kentucky. The date was April 14, 1863. He recovered in time to be captured on July 7, 1863 in Gladesville, VA, and was taken to Camp Chase on July 20, 1863. He was then taken to Johnson's Island on October 10, 1863. He took the oath on May 12, 1865, having been imprisoned the duration of the war.

Captain Robert Bates was the son of John W. Bates

and Sarah Waltrip. He was born on August 24, 1825. He was a brother to Private James Bates, Sgt. Jesse Bates, Uriah Bates and Private Martin Van Buren Bates. He married Elizabeth Bentley Bates (photo to the reader's right). Captain Bates enlisted on November 5, 1861, into the Confederate Army. He was in the 5th KY of the famed Orphan Brigade. He was at the Battle of Middle Creek. He served as a Captain in the 7th Confederate Cavalry, Company A. He died on September 24, 1921. Ms. Lola was fifteen years old and remembered several stories about her father. During visits (she did not like interviews), she revealed some information that was previously unknown and her knowledge assisted in the gathering of more data for the camp archives. Ms. Lola enjoyed gardening, cooking and her grandchildren. She was a big prankster and enjoyed a good laugh. She disliked 'republicans and publicity.' She was a very independent lady. She stated that she peddled eggs from her home in Knott County, Kentucky across the mountain to Neon, Kentucky (over 10 miles one way). She recalled with much affection a time when she was five days old that her daddy took a picture of her prior to his trip out west to look at a ranch he thought of purchasing. She treasured that picture of her being held by her father. She told stories of her father walking to Mt. Sterling driving cattle and geese to the auction sales. They would stop and camp, broiling meat over an open fire. The distance from their home to Mt. Sterling was at least 120 miles! Another story she shared with affection was of her brother Beckham Bates (Beckham Bates Elementary is named after him) being paid two dollars a day for hoeing, in the 'lead row' and that she refused to work unless she got the same amount of pay that her brother was receiving! She was the mother of seven and at the time of her passing had fifteen grandchildren and eighteen great grandchildren. She had 13 brothers and sisters that preceded her passing. They were Bobby, Hennie, Jess, Sam, Tandy Uriah, Joe, Ralph Booten, Beckham, Amanda Bates Calhoun, Minerva Bates Holbrook, Cleo Bates Baker, and Eliza Bates Collins. She will be missed by all but the circle is now unbroken. A letter of resolution has been sent to the family. Ladies and Gentlemen

let us tip our kepis and offer up a prayer for the family, as we honor one of our own; for *Lola Bates Honeycutt,* a real daughter has gone home:

<u>Thy Brothers Keeper</u>
David Chaltas

Who is a good neighbor? What constitutes an act of brotherly love? Where is the Good Samaritan? On April 19, 2005, I was returning from my college class and had an irresistible urge to call my childhood friends Ronnie and Hester. The week before, Ronnie's brother was found murdered in the woods of Pennsylvania and I was concerned about him. I called his house and to my horror his brother-in-law stated that Ronnie's son Ikie had been in a terrible wreck and had been flown to Knoxville, Tennessee. I called a parson who lives in Knoxville and explained to him what had happened and asked if he would pray for the family and the young man. I notified other prayer warriors and prayed for his recovery.

The next morning I called James, the Knoxville parson, and he gave me the sad news of the passing of Ikie. The parson simply stated that he would be available as needed and to let him know if there was anything he or his wife could do. Later that day I called Ronnie and discovered something of a man and woman that I thought I knew. He told me of two strangers that came to the hospital and sought him out. The strangers came up to him and introduced themselves and asked if they could stand watch with the family members present. They also asked if they could pray with them. They prayed for healing and the recovery of the young father of three. But the worst came to pass and the young man crossed through the turbid vale around 1:30 A.M.. Then Ronnie said that the strangers who would not leave his side asked him if there was anything else they could do for him. Being the man of character that Ronnie is, he asked for prayers for his beloved wife and his son's family. Ronnie gave the strangers a message of appreciation and love for their act of kindness and compassion. For the strangers were none other than our dear Parson James Smith and his wife Sherry. They sought no reward. They wanted no recognition. They were following the principles of their God. They acted out of love.

I loved them before this tragedy occurred, but now my heart is at their beckoning call. For they did not talk of love, they demonstrated it. They were the Good Samaritans. They were the good neighbors and showed brotherly love to strangers. They were led by works and showed us the great commandment of loving one another as ourselves. They are chaplains in the truest sense of the word and may we all emulate their piety and humbleness of spirit. We must lead by example and do all things out of love and compassion for our fellow man. Can we not also follow the example set forth by this couple and serve without thought of reward or recognition? Is that not what Christ did and bids us to do. Let us pray for one another, as we would do so for ourselves and remember the rule of rules: To do unto others, as you would have them do unto you. Sometimes God sends an angel unaware to others and it is then that we remember He said, "I will not leave you as orphans, I will come to you."

"POEMS OF THE PASSING"

Oh Momma, I Remember
David Chaltas
4/25/03

Oh Momma, I remember
The softness of your smile.
And though your light has ambered
You're with me all the while.

The things that you have taught me
Are written on the wind.
Nothing you could have bought me
Replaced the gifts within.

You said what was essential
Was carried by the heart.
Our time has been sequential:
Together then apart.

The one thing that you gave me
Lays buried in my chest.
That one gift is what saved me
And makes me do my best.

Oh mother, did I tell you
How much you meant to me?
The many times I failed you
But you forgave freely.

At times I feel your presence
Brush gently past my soul.
Precious motherly essence
That only children know.

Now the final curtain
In peace please go to rest.
There is one thing for certain,
You surely gave your best.

Rest high upon the mountain.
Your mission is complete.
Drink from the Master's fountain
And rest beside His feet.

Where You Rest Among the Shade of the Trees
David Chaltas

"I have no fear of dying,"
I heard my husband say.
"So dear, please stop your crying
And let me go my way."

"To die upon a Sunday.
Has always been my wish.
To dance upon the sun's rays
In evening hour's mist."

"Oh weep no more tomorrow.
This world is not my home.
Comfort lil' sorrel:
A warrior's going home"

"My soul to Him's delivered.
I truly long to be
Over across the river
And rest among the trees."

He left me here a crying
While down on bended knees.
Cross the river he's lying
Neath the shade of the trees.

At My Last End Day's
Bonnie Mae Baker

I looked out this morning
as far as I could see.
I saw a beautiful heaven,
shining down on me.
And, my mind began to wonder,
Just how long it would be,
Until my journey would be over,
And, the Lord would call for me.
But, I'll not worry about the problems,
Nor the price that we pay,
It started on Calvary on a hill far away.
Now, this valley may be chilly,
And, my body may be cold.
But, I won't have to worry,
It will never touch my soul.
He told me about the mansion,
And about the streets of gold,
But, words can't explain it,
the half that's never been told.
But, someday I will be there,
And then I'll be whole,
All my troubles will be over,
When those pearly gates unfold.

"Death is nothing more than a darkened sky that
hides the rays of the sun for a brief period of time."
David P. Chaltas

Autumn Moon
Shawana Slone

Autumn moon who hears my sweet sorrows,
Lend me your ear.
For I need to share with you the secrets I so dearly
fear.
What chance might come tomorrow.

My heart now soars like a dove in flight.
It finds such contentment in the present,
Yet it finds despair in the future's near sight.
I search for wisdom before your next crescent.

I have savored my dance in this life,
A beautiful waltz performed only briefly,
The missteps have been my strife,
The songs rhythm like a loosened bird seems to
flee.

Oh, Autumn moon what wonders I have seen.
How many friendships I've treasured.
How many slates have I washed clean?
Thankful for the love I could have never measured.

I grow old as fine wine,
Never wanting this body to die.
Ever clinging to what is mine.
Yet it is a fate, which I cannot deny.

When will the darkness of death take me to that
unknown place?
Will a restful peace dwell in my soul?
What will I face?
When will that final bell toll?

Shall I be remembered for what I have done?
Remembered for the kindness I have showed?
Remembered for the laughter and the fun?
Or forgotten like the gentle stream that flowed?

Daddy
Barbara Collins

We have rarely seen eye to eye.
But you were always by my side.
You were there looking over my shoulder.
You taught me how to take steps that were bolder.
If it happened that I should make a mistake,
You were there to gripe and complain
Quite honestly dad there was times
you almost drove me insane.
But now dad that we are older.
There is no longer a reason to be
such a tough little soldier.
You'll always be my daddy,
And I'll always be your daughter.
It is the advice you always gave.
It is in the words we find hard to say but always
knew.
You love me and I love you.

Letting Go
Shawana Slone

Life is spent in essence of letting go.

Letting go of childhood innocence so sweet,
Letting go of the sound of mother's heartbeat.
Letting go of baby dolls and toy cars,
Letting go while moving on with life's scars.

Letting go of adolescent years,
Letting go of puppy loves with woeful tears.
Letting go troubled words said,
Letting go while striving ahead.

Letting go of high school chums,
Letting go of milk and cookie crumbs,
Letting go of teenage games,
Letting go while constructing our own names.

Letting go of youthfulness so dear,
Letting go of childish fear,
Letting go of youthful dreams,
Letting go while remaining in the flow of things.

Letting go of memories of long ago,
Letting go of friends and foes,
Letting go of loved ones young and old,
Letting go while life around us unfolds.

Letting go of children as they grow,
Letting go of possessions cherished so,
Letting go of parents and security,
Letting go while searching for tranquility.

Letting go of words left unsaid,
Letting go of the life force upon a deathbed.
Letting go of all tomorrows,
Letting go while having no sorrows.

Yes, life is spent in essence of letting go.

Ronda Darlene
Bonnie Mae Baker

My little angel, you were so dear,
I still think about you, after all these years.

My arms still ache for you, just to hold you one
more time,
In losing you my little one, I nearly lost my mind.

I know you're in heaven, but it's hard to
understand,
God must have wanted you in His angel hand.

In my mind I can see you walking golden streets,
Knowing you are so happy, yet sometimes I still
weep.

A part of me left with you, a piece of my heart,
Someday I hope to see you, and never more depart.

My days are getting shorter, age catching up with
me,
Someday I hope to join you to spend eternity.

The Mirror
Barbara S. Collins

My senses are more vivid than ever as I look into
the mirror.
I see your face, looking back at me.
I hear your voice, calling out to me.
I can faintly smell your perfume around me.
As I close my eyes, I can almost feel your hand
touching mine.

105

Eager to see you, I open my eyes and realize that
you are not there.
I understand that you are not alive on earth but you
live through me
and I you'll always be in my heart.

My Mother
Barbara S. Collins

My mother was like no other,
she was my friend as well as being a great mother.
My mother had a love that made me feel safe,
She had a smile that look like a angel's face.
My mother was always on my side,
through thick and thin she remained my friend.
My mother took care of me through out my life,
she gave me courage to make choices that were
right.
Even though I lost my mother
her memory will live on through every step I take
and every decision that I will make.

Wishes Don't Come True
Alexis Bentley

It's been eight months now, nothing is getting
better.
I hope and pray to God that Jesus has met her.

I sit alone and think of the times we shared
And the little things she done that showed me she
cared.

There is nothing I could do nothing I could say.
Nothing I could dream that would bring her back
someday.

But I'll keep hoping, keep saying, keep dreaming
and keep praying
That I could see you just one last time, but wishes
like that don't come true.
But if I could have one wish it would be to tell her,
"I love you."

The Second Awakening
David Chaltas

We must not honor heroes
With dabbling of words.
We must never be like Nero;
Play fiddles while Rome burns.

Forgetting to remember
That they have given all.
The day of eleven September
When twin towers would fall.

We must keep candles burning
For all the world to see.
The land of free is learning
That freedom's never free.

Let us offer as a nation:
In unison we pray.
For values and salvation
We must never more stray.

For it is by our actions:
We are judged by the deeds
Not submitting to factions
Our conscience we must heed.

For our country and our God
Let's serve them again.
Let the heathen's fear to trod
On the hearts of free men.

Ode to 911
Chris Blanchard

Every generation has a moment to define them:
Pearl Harbor, Oklahoma City. This was our
moment. We shall not forget the people who gave
the ultimate sacrifice for freedom. The planes
crashed in New York City, D.C., and Pennsylvania.
Over 3,000 lives left us to be with the Lord, minus
19 who took the wrong elevator. This day five
years ago will live in infamy, lest we forget the true
heroes that day. The day the towers fell; the day the
Pentagon lost a side; the day a field had a smoking
hole. All where heroes of freedom: all shall
remember. Let us remember the heroes; remember
their lives; remember the moment; remember
9/11/01.

Twisted Shadows
Jessica Burke

Twisted shadows on the walls.
I see at night when darkness falls.
The clouds go gray, the sky goes black,
My blood runs cold, I lose the light.

I can't hear a sound, my heart stops beating
Suddenly it grabs me, and then I start bleeding.
When I look up, the shadows look me in the eye,
Then with a short gasp, I black out and die.

Someone
Jessica Burke

Someone you love and cherish, and hold when they
are dying
Someone you would die for, and make them smile
when they are crying

Someone you are there for, in ways both great and
small
And it seems like after you fight, is when you love
them most of all.

Someone you think you hate sometimes, and wish
that they were gone.
But when they are not with you, is when you miss
them most of all.

That is what a family is, and you might think that
this sounds mushy,
But if you have one, don't mess it up, because you
are so lucky.

For the Love of Billy
Jacob Burke

For the love of Billy
I will go home today,
Cherish all that I have,
And mean what I say.

For the love of Billy
I will go home today,
Kneel at my bed,
And begin to pray.

For the love of Billy
I will show more love,
I will show more respect,
To the great man above.

For the love of Billy
I will give more thought,
To the choices I make.
Like drugs and pot.

But Now She Sleeps
David Chaltas

As autumn ambers with the blanket of white, the
changing of the guard begins.
The fallen leaves nestle to her bosom as she lays
dormant before renewing herself.
She sings herself to sleep.
All's asleep; hibernating among the crystals.
The crisp air holds promises of spring while the
bitterness of the wind lifts the blanket in an attempt
to disrupt her slumber.
Yet she sleeps.
She turns and yawns as her warm breath hints of
tomorrow.
Yet she sleeps.
The frost glistens as the ice proclaims the promise
of her return by splintering under the weight of the
sun.
Yet she sleeps.
All cling to her with dreams of a fire crackling,
yielding its warmth to sustain life.
Yet she sleeps.
Soon her eyes will open and the blanket will be
folded, as those around respond to her beckoning.
But now she sleeps.

THE LAST ROLL CALL AND RECOVERY

We all possess the knowledge that life is temporal on this plain but we also intuitively know that life exists after death. This we know: life is a natural part of death. Death reminds us of our fragile nature and asks us to embrace life on life's terms. But when the sting of death arrives at our door due to the loss of a loved one, we experience grief, shock, denial, anger and bereavement that drain us of our essence. Only through faith can we slowly accept God's better judgment and realize that all must cross through that turbid vale to rest under the shade of the trees.

Death brings to our door many emotions. Kubler Ross described the stages of those dying in her highly acclaimed book, <u>On Death and Dying</u>, but each of us must walk that lonesome valley alone, save for a loving God that guides our path. But still shock, denial, disbelief, anger, depression, yearning, guilt and deep sadness permeates our senses. This is normal. This is the way of life and death. Grief is an outward expression of inward agony and pain. Mourning is that personal expression, that personal time that each of us must experience first hand in order to understand the private individual identity of death. But through it all we must possess a sense of love from the person departed and/or those that are being left behind. Love removes the fear, the doubt and faith guides the soul towards the final destination. Only time can remove the sharpness of the loss but be aware that the pang of loss will continue at times. Anniversaries, birthdays, special occasions and other personal days tend to bring us back to the longing of seeing the departed just one more time. In dreams they will come, as we reflect upon a simpler time, a happier time before the angel of death cast her dark shadow.

The feelings that you will experience are normal and common reactions to loss. You may not be prepared for the intensity and duration of your emotions or how swiftly your moods may change. It takes time to fully absorb the impact of a major loss. You never stop missing your loved one, but the pain eases after time and allows you to go on with your life.

Death is not easy. There are no magic words. There are no silver bullets. You will mourn and you will grieve. Mourning is the natural process that you must undergo in order to accept the loss. Mourning is very personal and is the amount of time that it takes to begin the healing process will depend upon your abilities to cope and express your feelings. Allow yourself the freedom to express your emotions, your feelings and fears. Find someone that you can talk to, join a grief group, share with relatives your feelings, talk openly and don't be afraid to cry. But most importantly, remember that God is there and He wants to ease your pain. Call upon His loving kindness and He will offer you a peace that will pass all understanding.

In Norman Vincent Peale's great little book entitled, Not Death At All, Doctor Norman V. Peale uses the birth process to describe the death process. It goes like this: When you are in the womb, approaching that appointed day of birth, you find that your world is about to totally change. Nestled within the confines of the nurturing mother, you have all of

112

your needs met but, as you get cramped into a tighter place because of your growth, you feel yourself becoming uncomfortable. Then the moment arrives in which you find yourself in the transition, caught between two worlds, hesitating. You say to yourself, I don't want to be born; I want to remain where I am! And after the laborious task is completed and you have crossed through that turbid vale into a new world, there to greet you is the most loving creature that God has ever created: your mother. Would the same God that afforded you such love and comfort at birth allow you to be alone after you pass to the other shore? Would that not be so out of character? He is a loving God, a gracious God; a God of the living and dying. He will be there for you as He promised. And in the mist you will see those loved ones of yesteryear. And there will be singing, and rejoicing and laughter and all shall know peace. May you find Him this day.

INFORMATION OF CUSTOMS AND RITUALS

The purpose of this segment is to offer the reader information of different practices, customs, rituals, and rights that are associated with death. Mourning in the mountains is our way of dealing with the pain of a loss. But other cultures as well as religions have their methodology of coping. Through education, maybe we can get a better understanding that death is universal and the rites of passage are based on the unique culture in which we reside and the wishes of the departed as well as the loved one.

Years ago it was expected that the body of the loved one would be brought back home for the visitation and funeral. The body was not left alone and someone sat up all night with the body. As time passed a new trend developed in that the body was brought to the families church and kept there for the visitation and funeral. Again the body was not left alone day or night. It is now common that the body be left at the funeral home for the visitation and funeral services. The family leaves the body and returns to their home each night.

It is now becoming more common for the visitation and the funeral to he held on the same day, rather than over a period of three days. The Bible speaks of a ritual of embalming the body and allowing the mourning to go on for forty days before burial. (Genesis 50:2-3)

EMBALMING

The methods to accomplish burial, and the meanings associated with it, are culturally determined. The burial process often requires the involvement of a functionary, who may be a professional, tradesperson, religious leader, servant, or even a member of the family. The embalming of Jacob in the Bible and the accounts recorded by Herodotus and archaeological discoveries of earlier cultures give evidence of the disposition of the dead.

In the sixteenth century with the discovery of the circulatory many attempts were made to embalm people. The ancient Egyptian process of embalming required seventy days to complete in contrast to today, which only requires a number of hours. In the United States it is estimated that four fifths of bodies are embalmed.

Embalming by definition is the replacement of normal body fluids and preserving chemicals. The embalming machine is the intravascular exchange of bodily fluids and preserving chemicals. Other creams, liquids, and/or sprays are used to give the appearance of normal skin coloration.

Some people ask, "Why embalm the dead body?" In many instances the process of dying leaves the body is in very repulsive state and the process of embalming and cosmetic reconstruction is necessary. Over seventy-five percent of funerals today involve Earth burial, which in most instances allow for viewing. The embalming process is necessary so the grievers can have time to view their loved one.

FINAL DISPOSITION

Burial is used in approximately seventy-five percent of the two point three (2.3) million American deaths annually. By law, every state has the right to establish rules and regulations to be observed by those arranging for burial that live in that state. Most cemeteries require that the casket be placed into some kind of receptacle or burial vault.

Entombment occurs in less than five percent of all final dispositions. It consists of placing the body (contained within a casket) into a building designed for this purpose. In some African societies, the deceased are buried underneath their homes/huts. In the Old American West, people were buried 6 feet under and typically today it is around four and one half feet (4 ½ feet) with eighteen (18) inches of dirt above the top of the vault. It is not necessary to put the person so far into the ground due to sealed caskets and vaults in contrast to pine boxes.

Cremation is burning the body. Buddhists and Hindus prefer this procedure. About twenty-five percent of Americans choose this method with Nevada leading the way with sixty-five percent.

After cremation the remains are collected, put in an urn/box, and then disposed of according to the wishes of the family. The ashes may be buried in a family plot or placed in a columbarium / or maybe kept in a home or church. One of my friends so loved the battlefield of Bridgeport, Alabama, that he wished to have his ashes spread over the field. His brother reenactors honored his wish and after an event, fired his ashes from the thirty plus artillery pieces, with over a thousand men firing their weapons in tribute to him. This was one of the most moving dedications that this fielder has ever witnessed.

CUSTOMS OF MAJOR RELIGIOUS GROUPS

Christian Customs

The Christian funeral service is primarily a worship service. It is common during the funeral service for hymns to be sung, scriptures from the Bible are read, and the obituary is read.

In the United States, the embalming process is practiced. Christian customs also do not prohibit autopsies or cremations. Funeral directors, members of the clergy, and/or cemetery directors, conduct the funeral. The family members make funeral arrangements with the professional assistance of a funeral home director.

Memorial services are becoming more common in America. A Memorial service is a religious service to honor the deceased but the deceased's body is not present. Family members of the deceased are expected to withdraw from most normal social gathering until after the funeral.

For the Roman Catholics and Protestants, a wake or visitation service will be held at the funeral home or church on the day before the funeral. The visitation lasts about five hours in duration. Friends of the family may view the body and visit family members during this time. In some parts of the US, it is customary for friends and neighbors to send flowers and food to the funeral home or church, which is a sign of respect. Roman Catholics also have a rosary service and/or a prayer service during wake.

The funeral typically takes place two to four days after the death. The funeral can be delayed so that family members who have to travel can attend the funeral. (This would not be allowed in a Jewish funeral). If cremation of the body is the form of body disposition, the cremation can be held after the funeral or before the memorial service.

After the funeral process, family members and close family friends go to the cemetery for graveside services. Often, after the burial, family members will gather for a meal.

Jewish Customs

It is Jewish custom to bury the deceased within twenty-four hours after the death. In the Jewish community it is customary that the body of a deceased person be treated with respect, washed wrapped in plain white cloth and put into a plain white coffin. Mourning can last for no longer than one year. (Lifecycle Events & Rituals http://www.jewishaz.com)

It is Jewish custom to be buried in a plain wooden coffin and without embalming except when local law says otherwise. Traditional Jewish customs does not allow for cremation or a viewing of the body. However, reform Judaism does allow for cremation. Members of the Jewish burial society cleanse the body. The cleansing/washing process is call *tahorah,* which means purification. The body is dressed in plain linen shrouds call *takhrikhim.*

Traditionally, for the bereaved, the Jewish mourning ritual begins with the tearing (rending) of clothes. For example, a parent cuts their left side of the clothing with a razor. For a spouse, sibling, or a child, the cut is made on the right side. However, the ripping of a black ribbon worn by family members has replaced the process of rending garments.

After a ritual feast, *Shiva* begins. Men are not allowed to shave for the first week. Family members are not allowed to bathe. The family receives while sitting on the floor or on low chairs. From the time of death until the burial is completed, family members are exempt from regular religious practices such as morning prayers. Family members are not allowed to engage in the following activities; drinking wine, eating meat, attending parties, and engaging in sexual intercourse.

The funeral service will consist of the recitation of psalms, a eulogy, and memorial prayer. The body is lowered into the grave in the interment service. This service consists of "an acclamation of God's justice, a memorial prayer, and the recitation of Qaddish-a doxology reaffirming the mourner's faith in God despite the fact of death."

After the *shiva*, family members are to refrain from participating in social gathering for thirty days after the death. If the deceased is a parent, the family members have to refrain from going to social gatherings for one year. Yahrzeit is the yearly commemoration of the person's death. On this day a memorial candle is lit in honor of the deceased.

Hindu Customs

It is Hindu customs for the body to be prepared by a person of the same gender. The body is laid out with the hands placed across the chest. The eyelids are closed. The body is anointed with oil and flower garlands are placed around the body.

Cremation is the most common and most preferred way to dispose of the body in Hindu religion. "In preparation for cremation, family members will construct a bier, consisting of a mat of woven coconut fronds stretched between two poles and supported by pieces of bamboo." The body is not placed in a casket. The body is placed on a bier, and carried from the deceased's home to the place of cremation. " The funeral procession will be led by the chief mourner- usually the eldest son- and will include musicians, drum players, and other mourners." The wife of the deceased remains at home during this time.

When the funeral procession reaches the place of cremation (usually a sacred river), the body will be immersed into the water of the sacred river. The priest will perform a brief ceremony. The body will be smeared with *ghi* (clarified butter) and placedon the pyre for burning. The chief mourner will light the pyre and they also bring the coals from the house of the deceased.

After the body has been cremated, mourners will wash themselves in the river in a rite of purification. They recite passages from scared texts. Three days after the cremation, few relatives of the deceased will return to the site of the cremation in order to gather the bones of the deceased. The Priest will read from sacred text. The bones of the deceased will be placed into a vase and given to the chief mourner who is obligated to place the remains into a sacred river.

"Between ten to thirty-one days, after the cremation, a *Shraddha* (elaborate ritual feast) is prepared for all mourners and priests who have taken part in the funeral rituals." "During the Shraddha, gifts are given to the *guru,* (religious teacher), the *purohita* (officiating priest), and other Brahmins (religious functionaries). The social status of the family will determine how elaborate the Shraddha will be-for the poor this ritual will last 8 to 10 hours, while the wealthy may give a Shraddha lasting several days. At the end of the Shraddha, the mourning period officially ends."

The traditional Hindu is the second most important religious ceremony. Only the Hindu wedding is considered more important than the funeral. The funeral and the Shraddha ceremony can be very expensive for a family sometimes even resulting in impoverishment for the family. In the Hindu religious culture, not giving the Shraddha creates more social problems for the family than financial problems.

In the Hindu religious culture, the husband is considered a god by the wife. The widow cannot remarry and is considered to be an outcast in society. In 1987, in India, a widow chose to be burned alive with her husband. This practice is called *Sati*. This practice has not been common since the early twentieth century. If the wife chooses to live, she had to "remain barefoot, sleep on the floor. And can never go out of the house because she would be slandered if seen talking to a man."

Buddhist Customs

Buddhist Death Rituals vary from country to country. Usually, Buddhist funerals are held at the Buddhist temple. The priest assists the families as they engage in the rite of passage. "Prayers of the priests illustrate the "lesson of death"- that life is vanity." At Buddhist funerals, the priest will read words from Buddha. Cremation is the most accepted form of body disposition in the Buddhist culture. However, earth burial is also practiced.

The family of the deceased will provide a ritual feast for the priests and mourners. The body is cleaned, dressed and placed into a casket. The casket is kept at the home or at the temple (*wat*) for the duration of three days. During the three days, monks will come in the evening to chant the Buddhist scriptures. Friends of the deceased will attend these services and will offer gifts of "floral tributes." On the fourth day, the body will be taken to the cremation site. "During the procession, a long white cotton cord is attached to the casket and eight monks together will carry the cord." In cities, the carriage is motorized, however in traditional funeral the members of the procession will pull the carriage.

At the cremation site, the family of the deceased will pose for pictures beside the casket. The obituary is read just prior to the cremation. A *dok mai chan* is given to all the mourners. A *dok mai chan* is a sandalwood flower with "one incense-stick and two small candles attached." Then, the mourners will come forward and place their *dok mai chan* before the casket.

"The chairman of the ceremony" lights the fire and the casket is consumed. "The next morning, the ashes are gathered and made into a shape of a human being with the head facing east."

In the Hindu religious culture, sorrow or mourning is not emphasized. The funeral is more of a social gathering; people are expected to enjoy the company of others. Often, there is entertainment, such as dancing and musical performances. The focus of happiness rather than on sorrow is thought to "assist the bereaved to conceptualize a happy and pleasant paradise in which the deceased will reside."

Muslim Customs

Muslims have a ritual surrounding death that requires that the body remain covered at all times. Only health workers that are of the same sex as the deceased should touch the body. Muslims are buried within twenty-four hours of death. Sometimes coffins are not used and the body is placed directly into the ground. (Guide for Health Workers on the rituals surrounding death and dying http://www.beaumont.ie/CAN/dda.htm).

FAMOUS EPITAPHS

Les Moore buried in Tombstone: Here lies Lester Moore four slugs from a 44 no Less no more.

George Washington: Looking into the portals of eternity teaches that the brotherhood of man is inspired by God's word; then all prejudice of race vanishes away.

Jesse James: Murdered by a traitor and a coward whose name is not worthy to appear here.

Jefferson Davis: An American Soldier and defender of the constitution.

Unknown Soldier: To save your world you asked this man to die: would this man, could he see you now, ask why?

Benjamin Franklin: The body of Benjamin Franklin, printer (like the cover of an old book, its contents worn out, and stript of its lettering and gilding) lies here, food for worms. Yet the work itself shall not lost, for it will, as he believed, appear once more in a new and more beautiful edition, corrected and amended by its Author

FINAL THOUGHTS VIA SAYINGS

"And when the last red man shall have perished, and the memory of my tribe shall become a myth among the white men, these shores will swarm with the invisible dead of my tribe; and when our children's children think themselves alone in the field, the store, the shop, upon the highway, or in the pathless woods, they will not be alone. Let him be just and deal kindly with my people, for the dead are not powerless. Dead, did I say? There is no death, only change of worlds." *Chief Seattle*

"But in the night of death hope sees a star, and listening love can hear the rustle of a wing." *Ingeresoll*

"I believe there are two sides to the phenomenon known as death, this side where we live, and the other side where we shall continue to live. Eternity does not start with death. We are in eternity now." *Norman Vincent Peale*

"Death is no more than passing from one room into another. But there's a difference for me, you know. Because in that other room I shall be able to see." *Helen Keller*

"What we have done for ourselves alone dies with us; what we have done for others and the world remains and is immortal." *Albert Pike*

"I have been driven many times upon my knees by the overwhelming conviction that I had nowhere else to go." *Attributed to Lincoln*

"So live your life that the fear of death can never enter your heart. Trouble no one about their religion; respect others in their view, and demand that they respect yours. Love your life, perfect your life, beautify all things in your life. Seek to make your life long and its purpose in the service of your people. Prepare a noble death song for the day when you go over the great divide. Always give a word or a sign of salute when meeting or passing a friend, even a stranger, when in a lonely place. Show respect to all people and grovel to none. When you arise in the morning give thanks for the food and for the joy of living. If you see no reason for giving thanks, the fault lies only in yourself. Abuse no one and no thing, for abuse turns the wise ones to fools and robs the spirit of its vision. When it comes your time to die, be not like those whose hearts are filled with the fear of death, so that when their time comes they weep and pray for a little more time to live their lives over again in a different way. Sing your death song and die like a hero going home."
Chief Tecumseh, Shawnee Nation

"You shall know the truth and the truth shall set you free."

www.ingramcontent.com/pod-product-compliance
Lightning Source LLC
Chambersburg PA
CBHW022153080426
42734CB00006B/415